CANADIAN
Wineries

CANADIAN
Wineries

Text by Tony Aspler
Photography by Jean-François Bergeron/Enviro Foto

FIREFLY BOOKS

A FIREFLY BOOK

Published by Firefly Books Ltd. 2013

First Printing

Publisher Cataloging-in-Publication Data (U.S.)
Aspler, Tony-
    Canadian wineries / Tony Aspler ; Jean-François Bergeron, photographer.
[272] p. : col. photos., ; cm.
Includes index.
Summary: A detailed, illustrated guide to Canada's top wineries.
ISBN-13: 978-1-77085-244-0 (pbk.)
1. Wineries—Canada. 2. Wine industry—Canada. I. Bergeron, Jean-François. II. Title.
641.22/0971 DC23   TP559.C2A875CW 2013

Library and Archives Canada Cataloguing in Publication
Aspler, Tony
    Canadian wineries / Tony Aspler ; Jean-François Bergeron, photographer.
Includes index.
ISBN 978-1-77085-244-0
1. Wineries—Canada. 2. Wine and winemaking—Canada. I. Bergeron, Jean-François. II. Title.
TP559.C3A856
2013   663'.200971   C2013-901229-X

Published in the United States by
Firefly Books (U.S.) Inc.
P.O. Box 1338, Ellicott Station
Buffalo, New York 14205

Published in Canada in 2013 by
Firefly Books Ltd.
50 Staples Avenue, Unit 1
Richmond Hill, Ontario L4B 0A7

Cover and interior design and typesetting:
Gareth Lind, LINDdesign
Printed in Canada

The publisher gratefully acknowledges the financial support for our publishing program by the Government of Canada through the Canada Book Fund as administered by the Department of Canadian Heritage.

Acknowledgements

To the young canadians who will discover our terroirs and wines elaborated with passion.

I would like to express my grateful recognition to the individuals and organizations who provided invaluable support during my travels in Canada's wine regions: Denise Le Gal, Tourism Vancouver Island; Deborah Kulchiski, Tourism Langley; Catherine Frechette, Tourism Kelowna; Tracy Reis, Tourism Penticton; Beth Garrish, Oliver Tourism Association; Jo Knight, Destination Osoyoos; the team at the Wine Council of Ontario — Linda Watts, Regina Foisey, Magdalena Kaiser-Smit; Nicole Leaper, Ontario Tourism Marketing Partnership Corporation; Chris Ryan, Tourism Windsor Essex County; Dominique Harmegnies and Julien Cormier, Tourisme Québec; Alain Larouche and Danie Béliveau, ATR Cantons de l'Est; Guylaine Beaudoin and Pierre Genesse, CLD Brome-Missisquoi; Nadège Marion and Robert Brisebois, Vignobles Les Trois Clochers; and Pamela Wamback, Tourism Nova Scotia.

I must also acknowledge the immense contribution of all the winery owners, winemakers and staff members who provided me with the best experience a photojournalist could have.

Merci to Layne and Rod in Toronto and to Sylvie and Robin in British Columbia for our long-lasting friendship. Thanks to the team at Firefly Books: Lionel Koffler, Michael Mouland, Michael Worek and Jacqueline Hope Raynor, and to editor Tracy C. Read, proofreader Charlotte DuChene and designer Gareth Lind for your dedication and hard work.

I'd also like to thank my wife, Hélène Savard, and my daughter, Marie Savard-Bergeron, for their love and continuing support throughout this challenging project.

— Jean-François Bergeron

For my friend Donald Ziraldo, whose consummate marketing put Canadian wine on the map.

In addition to Jean-François' list of thanks to individuals and institutions who have assisted us on this project, I would like to thank Debi Pratt of Inniskillin, to whom I could turn when I needed information from Constellation wineries in Ontario and British Columbia. Thanks also to my wine writer colleagues, John Schreiner and Tim Pawsey in British Columbia and Sean Wood in Nova Scotia. Finally, to my wife Deborah, to whom I entrusted the research while I was travelling.

— Tony Aspler

An early-morning October fog rolls over the vineyards of Québec's Vignoble Les Trois Clochers, following spread.

Contents

Introduction

THERE WERE, AT the time this book went to press, some 560 wineries across Canada. Most make their wines from grapes grown in the region; many produce orchard and berry fruit wines, and some make cider and mead. By the time you read these words, there may well be dozens of new wineries across the country as more and more Canadians succumb to the romantic lure of owning a winery.

You may be surprised to know that wine, whether grape- or fruit-based, is made in every Canadian province. The only regions not engaged in winemaking are the territories in the Far North; and with global warming, who knows—in the future, we might just see a Nunavut Riesling or a Northwest Territories Baco Noir.

In preparing this book, photographer Jean-François Bergeron and I travelled across Canada, at different times and during different seasons, from 2005 until publication, to document in pictures and prose what our wineries do best. In making a final selection as to whom we should include, we had to make some hard decisions. So, what were the criteria we used to determine which wineries should be featured here?

First, we were adamant that wine quality across the winery's portfolio and sustained quality from vintage to vintage should be prime considerations. Those criteria precluded the inclusion of very new wineries, such as Pearl Morissette in Jordan, Ontario, and Culmina Family Estate in Oliver, British Columbia, both of which are already making stellar wines.

Second, the wineries in question had to be historically

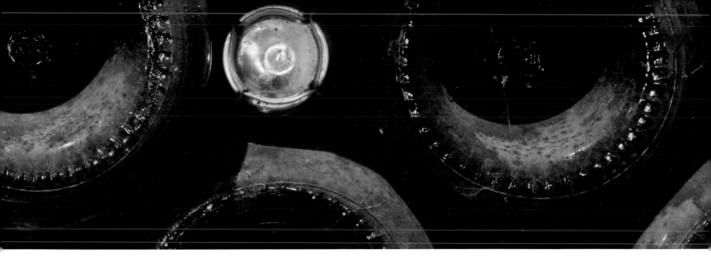

significant and have made a marked influence on the direction and style of the wines in their region. A classic example is Inniskillin, which created a global market for Canadian Icewine.

Third, since this is a pictorial record of the best that Canada has to offer in the world of wine, there had to be an aesthetic appeal to the property and its setting. For many years, wineries were started on farms, where on-site barns were converted into fermenting facilities. Over the past 15 years or so, winery owners have invested in custom-built facilities that include gravity-flow operations to improve wine quality, and many of these structures are architecturally exciting in their own right. In designing facilities that blend seamlessly into the countryside, these winemakers have been as respectful to the landscape as they have to their terroir. In addition, they have preserved the heritage aspects of their properties.

We have also taken into consideration the style and character of wines grown in the four provinces featured in this book. Each has its own personality, based on climate and terroir. For instance, you can't make a comparison of wines grown near Québec City with those grown in British Columbia's Osoyoos.

While restricting ourselves to portraying the number of "best wineries in Canada" — with a nod to each wine-growing province — we have taken the liberty of including other details of wineries and personalities that did not make the final edit but which nevertheless have something special to offer wine lovers. Ultimately, you may not agree with our choices, but that only speaks to how good wines grown in Canadian soil have become in a relatively short time. Cheers!

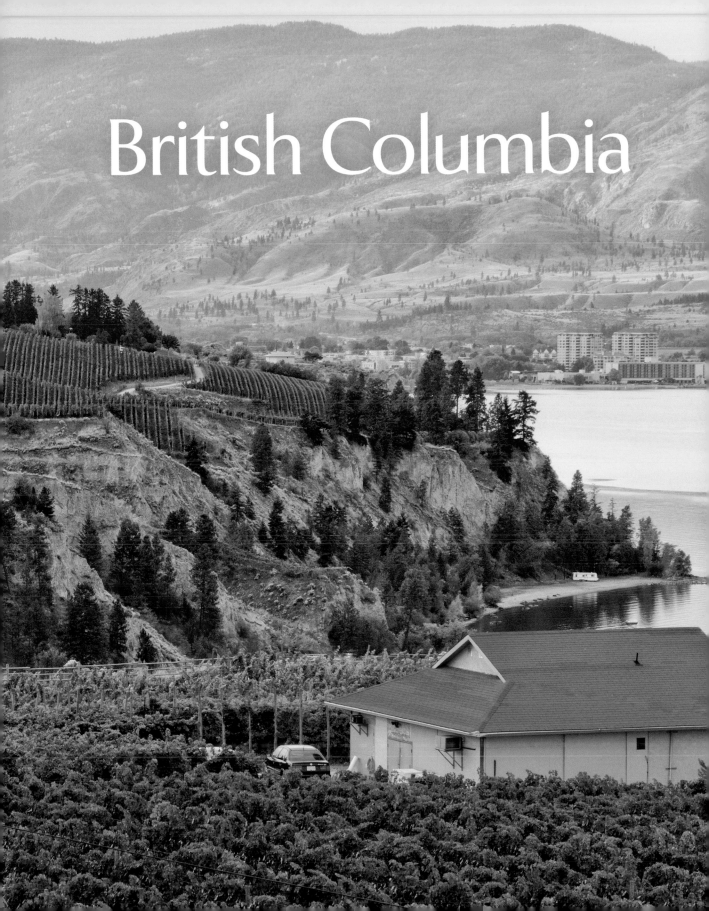

British Columbia

British Columbia

Land of Forests, Mountains and Vines

A T 95 MILLION HECTARES, British Columbia's total land mass is larger than that of France and Germany combined. To date, a mere 4,000 hectares of this mountainous and forested province are planted to vines, but that number is growing as new wine enthusiasts open their own wineries.

Given its geography, British Columbia resembles Chile writ small. It's a vertical wine region stretching from Salmon Arm in the north to the Washington state border. The range in temperature and rainfall, as well as in soil type, is enormous. The town of Oliver boasts 318 days with temperatures over 18°C; Cowichan Bay on Vancouver Island has a mere 52 days over that mark. Thus the island and the northern Okanagan feature early-ripening hybrids, while Oliver and the Osoyoos region can ripen Bordeaux varieties such as Cabernet Sauvignon and Merlot and the Rhône variety Syrah. The grape varieties planted through the province are divided almost evenly between white and red, with Merlot dominating, followed by, in order of importance, Pinot Gris, Chardonnay, Pinot Noir and Cabernet Sauvignon.

As an Ontarian, I am grieved to admit it, but British Columbia has the most beautiful winescape in Canada. The hills and mountains that enclose the Okanagan and Similkameen valleys offer vistas of incredible beauty, none more spectacular than the Naramata Bench, where vineyards seem to float above the blue waters of the lake like a green eiderdown. The Fraser Valley reminds me of Western Australia, with its farms and trees, while Vancouver Island — its remarkable vineyards

Mt. Lehman Winery's Fraser Valley vineyards are flanked by coastal forest, with the icy profile of Mount Baker in the distance, opposite, while the southern Okanagan Valley's Hester Creek Estate shows off a touch of Tuscany, above. The previous spread pictures a cool October morning on the Naramata Bench, overlooking Lake Okanagan.

13

tucked into forest clearings — is a delight to discover.

I wonder whether Father Charles Pandosy saw a wine future for this land of forests and mountains in 1859, when he created the first non-Native settlement on the banks of L'Anse au Sable (now Mission Creek). Today, the site bears the postal address of 3685 Benvoulin Road, Kelowna. Sometime in the early 1860s, Pandosy planted a vineyard to supply wine to his Oblate mission and the settlement. In the process, he became the father of the B.C. wine industry.

More than any other institution, the Catholic Church is responsible for today's flourishing international wine industry — and indeed the existence of every other alcoholic beverage industry, from beer to brandy and liqueurs. The monks of Europe kept the vineyards alive during the Dark Ages, and their missionaries carried vine cuttings along with their Bibles when they established religious settlements in the New World. Wine was needed to celebrate mass, and wherever priests set down roots, they planted vines. British Columbia was no exception.

But the farmers who followed the example of Father Pandosy were more interested in fruit crops such as apples, peaches and apricots than in grapes. Although there were experimental plantings as early as 1905, the first commercial vineyard in the province was planted by W.J. Wilcox only in 1920, some 88 kilometres north of Kelowna, at Salmon Arm. The most northerly limit of wine growing in the province, it was not the most promising place to start. This small plot yielded such grape varieties as Concord, Niagara, Delaware

and Agawam, all intended for eating rather than fermenting. Six years later, a grower named Jim Creighton planted a small vineyard in Penticton, an area that would ultimately prove to be one of the best sites for grape growing along the shores of Okanagan Lake.

In fact, the first wines in British Columbia were not made from grapes but from loganberries that flourished on the Saanich Peninsula of Vancouver Island. These beverages, made by the Growers' Wine Company, bore names such as Slinger's Logan and Logana. Only a few intrepid souls turned their attentions to wine grapes. Charles Casorso of Kelowna (the great-uncle of winemaker Ann Sperling) was a pioneer wine grower who planted a vineyard on a 14-hectare property at Rutland, near Kelowna, in 1925. The following year, a farmer by the name of Jesse Willard Hughes, encouraged by Hungarian oenologist Dr. Eugene Rittich, bought an 18.2-hectare vineyard in Kelowna, near the Pandosy mission, and planted vines that had been locally propagated. Hughes also purchased an 8-hectare site east of Kelowna, on Black Mountain. The larger vineyard in Kelowna prospered to such an extent that, four years later, wines made from these grapes were vinified at the Growers' Wine Company in Victoria. Encouraged by his success, Hughes expanded his Kelowna vineyard to 122 hectares; however, the experiment at Black Mountain proved a disaster when the vines were wiped out by winterkill (frost).

In 1930, when Rittich was hired as the winemaker for the Growers' Wine Company, a freak of nature gave the fledgling industry the boost it needed. Successive abundant

Richard and Jitske Kamphuys' Ancient Hill Estate Winery in Kelowna offers a warm welcome.

harvests of apples caused a glut on the market, and many farmers were forced to tear out their orchards and plant grapes instead. Growers' was paying $100 a tonne for grapes (compared with $65 a tonne in Ontario), while apples were left rotting under the trees. "A cent a pound or on the ground," was the farmers' anguished cry. "A dollar a box or on the rocks."

Then, at the height of the Depression in 1932, an immigrant Italian winemaker named Guiseppe Ghezzi came to Kelowna with the idea of creating a winery expressly to use the worthless apple crop. The same idea had also occurred to local hardware store owner William Andrew Cecil Bennett, who discussed

just such a possibility with his neighbour on Kelowna's main street, an Italian grocer named Pasquale "Cap" Capozzi. Both men were teetotallers, but they joined with Ghezzi to form a company called Domestic Wines and By-Products that would manufacture not only wines but a gamut of products, including "apple cider...brandy, alcohol, spirits of all kinds, fruit juices, soft drinks, fruit concentrates, jelly jams, pickles, vinegar, tomato paste, tomato catsup, tomato juice and by-products of every kind."

Bennett and Capozzi set about raising money to finance their new operation. At a

October is harvest time at the Seven Stones Winery in the Similkameen Valley.

time when soup kitchens meant more to the public than wineries, they began selling shares in the company for one dollar. They raised $4,500, and although they were undercapitalized, they bought fermenting tanks and other equipment to begin this multi-faceted business. In September 1932, they took up residence in an old rented building on Kelowna's Smith Avenue. The following year, they hired Ghezzi's son Carlo as winemaker to complete their staff of eight employees. The debonair Guiseppe Ghezzi stayed long enough to set up the winery before migrating to California, where he established a sparkling-wine plant.

Domestic Wines and By-Products' initial production included four apple-based wines — Okay Red, Okay Clear, Okay Port and Okay Champagne. But the products were far from "okay." Even the company's official history records show that the wines were "a bitter disappointment." Many bottles refermented on liquor store shelves and had to be thrown out. Liquor stores were reluctant to stock the ill-famed domestic wines, and people were reluctant to buy them: "Sales in the company's first full year of operation were a disaster, amounting to a mere few thousand dollars."

After three years of ineffectual competition against the genuine wines of the Growers'

Company, Bennett and Capozzi realized that B.C. consumers did not want apple wines. They switched from local grapes to California grapes, which had superior ripeness and sugar levels. Soon, other companies such as Growers' and the Victoria Wineries on Vancouver Island also bought grapes from California, perpetuating the fiction of making domestic wines by including whatever local grapes were available at the time — a practice that still persists.

With the change in product, the former apple winery needed a change in name. In 1936, the directors chose a phonetic spelling of the Indian place name where the company was located: Calona Wines Limited. Okay Clear apple wine became Calona Clear grape wine, a white semi-sweet product whose label read ominously, "When Fully Mature: About 28% Proof Spirit."

In 1940, W.A.C. Bennett left Calona Wines to pursue a career in politics. One year later, he was elected to B.C.'s Legislative Assembly, and he sold his shares to Capozzi. When Bennett became premier of the province in 1952, he took a serious look at the wine industry he had helped to create. If the wineries were to sell their products through the government-controlled liquor stores, he argued, they should do their part in promoting the grape-growing industry. In 1960, the B.C. government passed a law stating that wines vinified in the province had to contain a minimum percentage of locally grown grapes. Because only 237 hectares were under vines in the Okanagan Valley, that figure was set at 25 percent. To encourage the planting of new vineyards, the liquor board stated that the quota would rise to 50 percent in 1962 and 65 percent by 1965.

A chalkboard at Kelowna's Summerhill Pyramid Winery signals a cheery welcome to visitors.

In the early 1960s, farmers in the Okanagan Valley began planting French and American hybrids (Okanagan Riesling, De Chaunac, Maréchal Foch, Verdelet, Rougeon, Chelois and Baco Noir), and within four years, the total acreage had risen by 400 percent. In 1961, Andrew Peller, aged 57 and already a successful brewer and icemaker in Ontario, built a spanking new winery for Andrés at Port Moody. Six years later, a company called Southern Okanagan Wines of Penticton opened for business, but it soon changed its name to Casabello. At the same time, the beautifully situated Mission Hill Winery was

The hilly terrain bordering Nk'Mip Cellars, where animal-protection signs dot the property, is one of the few true desert ecosystems in Canada. The old Haynes homestead, opposite, located near Osoyoos, recalls the area's early-20th-century ranching activity.

built on a ridge overlooking Okanagan Lake at Westbank. This facility was acquired in 1969 by the ebullient construction king and brewer Ben Ginter, who promptly renamed it — with characteristic flamboyance, if little understanding of consumer sophistication — Uncle Ben's Gourmet Winery, putting a portrait of himself on his labels. Among the products Ginter went on to market were such pop wines as Fuddle Duck and Hot Goose.

From 1974 to 1979, growers turned their attention to grape varieties imported from California and Washington. Experimental plantings of Cabernet Sauvignon, Merlot, Chenin Blanc, Gewürztraminer, White and Grey Riesling, Sémillon and Chardonnay were evaluated at 18 sites throughout the Okanagan. In 1975, on the advice of Germany's renowned grape researcher Dr. Helmut Becker, George Heiss, the founder of Gray Monk Winery, brought in Auxerrois, Pinot Gris and Gewürztraminer from France to plant in his Okanagan Centre vineyard.

Wine growers are made from hardy stock, and in spite of initial setbacks, they learned how to keep vines alive over the winter months and where to plant certain varieties for the best results. Today, at the time of writing, there are 237 grape, fruit and honey wineries in British Columbia in five designated viticultural areas — Fraser Valley, Okanagan Valley, Similkameen Valley, Vancouver Island and Gulf Islands, and Shuswap and Northern British Columbia. The critical mass of wineries is located along the 135-kilometre length of Lakes Okanagan, Skaha and Osoyoos, a region that accounts for more than 80 percent of the wineries in the province. I say, "at the time of writing," because there are more wineries to come. Everyone, it seems, wants to get into the wine business in British Columbia.

The most southerly reaches, from Oliver to Osoyoos, are part of Canada's only desert, where the presence of rattlesnakes is just one of the challenges faced by wine growers. If Father Pandosy could look down and see his vision fulfilled, he might well raise a glass of ambrosia to the ever-growing roster of winery owners of British Columbia who have proclaimed the town of Oliver the "Wine Capital of Canada."

Black Hills Estate Winery

Winemaker Graham Pierce.

Black Hills Estate Winery
30880 Black Sage Road
RR 1, Site 52, Comp 22
Oliver, BC V0H 1T0
(250) 498-0666
blackhillswinery.com

THE ORIGINAL BLACK HILLS winery, founded in 1999, was housed in a Quonset hut that looked like an over-turned rowboat beached on the sunburnt hills of the Black Sage Bench. A couple of planks supported on barrels served as the tasting room. Before that, the hut had been used to build demolition derby cars. By the time new owners acquired the winery and its 11 hectares of vineyard in 2008, Black Hills had already achieved cult status with local wine lovers, thanks to winemaker Senka Tennant's Bordeaux-inspired Nota Bene red blend and a Sémillon/Sauvignon Blanc called Alibi. In the 2005 vintage, Senka produced the first Carmenère (the flagship variety of Chile) to be grown and vini-fied in Canada.

The new owners — a board of five that included actor Jason Priestley — invested heavily, encouraging Penticton-based architect Nick Bevanda to design and build a state-of-the-art winery. The board's confidence was rewarded when in 2008, Black Hills became the first winery to win the Lieu-tenant Governor of British Columbia Award for architectural excellence. Four years later, the winery opened its $1 million ultra-modern 280-square-metre wine shop and tasting room. Perched on a knoll at the edge of a 5.7-hectare vineyard the company purchased in 2011, this dramatic modern structure commands a great view of the valley.

In addition to the legacy wines of Senka Tennant, wine-maker Graham Pierce has added a Chardonnay and the Rhône varietals Syrah and Viognier to Black Hills' portfolio. In 2012, Graham introduced a new series of more affordable wines, called Cellarhand Red and Cellarhand White, as second labels to Nota Bene and Alibi. A 225-litre barrel of Nota Bene sold at a charity auction for $19,000.

Blasted Church Vineyards

Blasted Church proprietors Chris and Evelyn Campbell, both former Vancouver accountants, offer an amusing back story to explain their winery's name. In 1929, a wooden church in Fairview, British Columbia, was to be dismantled and reassembled in Okanagan Falls, some 26 kilometres away. With the help of the parish priest, who lit the fuse, miners deployed several sticks of dynamite to loosen the wooden nails that held the church rafters together. The controlled blast toppled the steeple, but the rest of the building was unharmed. Blasted Church winemaker Mark Wendenburg has a large portfolio of wines with lighthearted names that echo the liturgical theme — a blend of varietals, Mixed Blessings; a meritage, Nothing Sacred; and a port named Amen.

Blasted Church Vineyards
378 Parsons Road
RR 1, Site 32, Comp 67
Okanagan Falls, BC V0H 1R0
(877) 355-2686 · (250) 497-1125
blastedchurch.com

Blue Mountain Vineyard and Cellars

Blue Mountain Vineyard and Cellars
2385 Allendale Road
Okanagan Falls, BC V0H 1R2
(250) 497-8244
bluemountainwinery.com

A SELF-TAUGHT WINEMAKER, Ian Mavety is an industry maverick who has been growing grapes since 1971. After selling his fruit to B.C.'s commercial wineries for two decades, Ian opened his own facility in 1991. Today, Blue Mountain owns more than 35 hectares of vineyards in Okanagan Falls, where a 2.5-metre electrified fence encompasses the property to keep out deer and discourage the black bears that occasionally try to dig their way under it.

There's a certain exclusivity about this family enterprise, which is run by Ian, his wife Jane and their son Matt, who studied viticulture and oenology in New Zealand. Matt heads up the winemaking team, while his wife Christie is in charge of sales and marketing. Truly an estate winery, Blue Mountain crushes only its own organically farmed grapes. The inspiration for the vineyard's narrow and highly select portfolio of products is Burgundy and Champagne. The Mavetys produce Pinot Noir, Gamay, Pinot Gris, Pinot Blanc and Chardonnay, and in 2009, they introduced their first Sauvignon Blanc. The new section of the vineyard is densely planted after the style of Burgundy to ensure the vines compete and put down deep roots for nourishment.

The view from the access road to the winery is one of the most photographed of B.C.'s panoramas, incorporating granite mountains, pine forests, Vaseaux Lake and an undulating carpet of Blue Mountain's vineyards. The Mavetys also produce excellent sparkling wines and two qualities of varietals — Cream label and Striped label (Reserve). Blue Mountain's wines are available only at the winery — a model of cleanliness and precision — or in select restaurants. The portfolio across the board is top-notch, and I would rank Blue Mountain as one of the best wineries in British Columbia.

Burrowing Owl Estate Winery

Chris Wyse and his sister Kerri Wyse-McNolty, the happy guardians of the domaine.

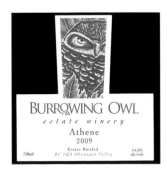

**Burrowing Owl
Estate Winery**
100 Burrowing Owl Place
RR 1, Site 52, Comp 20
Oliver, BC V0H 1T0
(877) 498-0620
(250) 498-0620
burrowingowl.ca

LOCATED ON A sandy plateau at the northernmost reaches of the Sonora Desert, Burrowing Owl sits like a stately galleon in a sea of vines. The 45-hectare vineyard was planted in 1993 and has been developed with an eco-friendly philosophy. Proprietor Jim Wyse named it after the endangered long-legged burrowing owl whose habitat is protected here — the winery's tasting fees are donated to the Burrowing Owl Conservation Society.

The staff, too, are highly conscious of the ecological imperative of the land they work. More than 100 bluebird boxes have been placed around the vineyard, and two bat nurseries have been installed so that their residents can feed on grape-defiling insects, rather than the vineyard workers having to do battle with chemical pesticides. In spring, the ground-nesting meadowlarks are protected by barriers to prevent farm machinery and vineyard workers from inadvertently destroying them. Even the rattlesnakes that seek shade under the vines are carefully relocated.

Constructed in 1998, the southwestern-style gravity-flow winery building overlooks Osoyoos Lake at its northern end. If you climb up to the walkway along the square tower above the building, you're rewarded with a spectacular 360-degree vista of the vineyards, granite cliffs and the lake.

Burrowing Owl has built an enviable reputation for its reds. Initially, the winery offered Cabernet Sauvignon and Merlot for red wines, Chardonnay and Pinot Gris for white. Cabernet Franc was added in 1998, Pinot Noir in 1999 and Syrah in 2000. In fact, the building was originally designed as a 12,000-case facility, but the demand for Owl wines is so great that it now produces 40,000 cases. An ideal place to taste winemaker Bertus Albertyn's wines by the glass is the Sonora Room Restaurant, one of the finest restaurants in the valley.

In 2006, Jim Wyse opened a 12-unit guest house adjacent to the winery with a wine lounge and its own cellar. Burrowing Owl winery, which is now run by Jim's children, son Chris and daughter Kerri Wyse-McNolty, also owns vineyard property in the adjacent Similkameen Valley.

CedarCreek Estate Winery

CedarCreek Estate Winery
5445 Lakeshore Road
Kelowna, BC V1W 4S5
(250) 764-8866
cedarcreek.bc.ca

EDARCREEK SITS LIKE a gleaming white Mediterranean palace above the eastern shore of Okanagan Lake, its garden terrace restaurant commanding a spectacular view of the water. With its block of cherished Pinot Noir vines, the home vineyard undulates down to the water's edge. The sloping 19-hectare vineyard above the terrace faces Quails' Gate winery on the opposite shore. In addition, the Fitzpatrick family owns the 16-hectare Greata Ranch winery in Peachland (formerly B.C.'s largest apple orchard) and vineyard properties in Desert Ridge and Haynes Creek in Osoyoos.

One of the oldest wineries in the Okanagan, CedarCreek traces its history to 1978, when it was one of the valley's original eight estate wineries. That year, a geologist-turned-fruit-farmer named David Mitchell opened the doors of Uniacke Cellar, a facility he had named after his grandmother. The Uniacke name dates back to 14th-century Ireland, when a member of the Fitzgerald clan was recognized as being "without peer" or "unique" for his services to his king. Fitzgerald took the

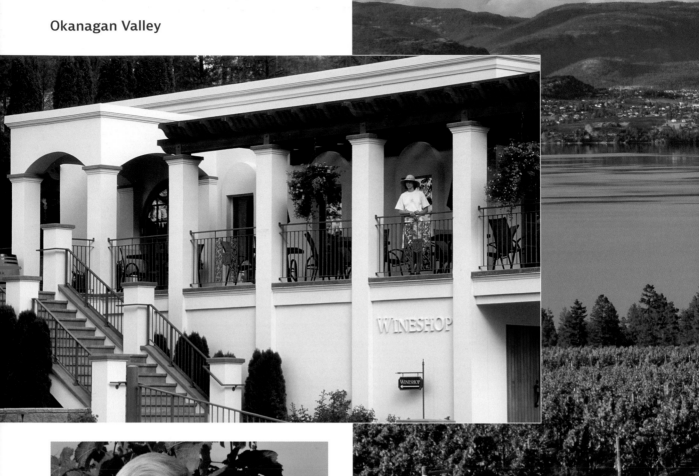

Senator Ross Fitzpatrick.

compliment to heart and used it as his family name, one that eventually migrated to Nova Scotia in 1775 with settlers from County Cork. To this day, there is still a Nova Scotian community named Mount Uniacke.

In 1986, Senator Ross Fitzpatrick bought the property and six years later injected $4 million into expanding the facilities, burrowing into a hillside to create a 420-square-metre barrel

room. The winery's style is distinctly Californian, thanks to the guidance of two California winemakers since 1998, but it is currently the domain of Australian Darryl Brooker, who created fine wines at Flat Rock Cellars and Hillebrand in Ontario before moving west in 2010. Darryl's Aussie approach can be seen in the Shiraz/Cabernet he's introduced to the portfolio since his arrival.

The seminal event in the story of CedarCreek goes back to 1993, when then-winemaker Ann Sperling won a platinum medal at the Okanagan Wine Festival for her 1992 Merlot Reserve—the first and only time such an award has been made. This triumph initiated CedarCreek's flagship Platinum Reserve Series in 1998.

La Frenz Winery

La Frenz Winery
1525 Randolf Road
Penticton, BC V2A 8T5
(250) 492-6690
lafrenzwinery.com

O F ALL THE vintners in British Columbia and perhaps in Canada, Australian Jeff Martin may have the longest history of continuous winemaking: The 2012 vintage was his 42nd crush. Jeff began his career in his native Australia at the age of 18 and worked his way up to become the chief red winemaker at McWilliam's Wines. He was based at the company's Beelbangera facility in Riverina for 14 years before he, his wife Niva and their two young daughters immigrated to Canada in 1994.

Jeff made an immediate impact on the Canadian wine scene with the bold Pinot Noirs and Chardonnays he produced at Quails' Gate before he opened his own small winery on the Naramata Bench, near Penticton, in 1999. The winery is named after his grandfather, who was born in Schleswig

Holstein. La Frenz's new Aussie-style tasting room, with its shaded pergola and floor-to-ceiling windows, is set in a sea of vines and offers a fabulous view from the patio across the lake toward Summerland and Peachland — a landscape snapshot that once graced the back of the old Canadian $100 bill.

The winery owns 16 hectares of vineyard land, each dramatically named — Rattlesnake Vineyard, above the winery at an elevation of 457 metres, grows mainly white varietals and some Merlot; Desperation Hill Vineyard ("named by Niva after driving from top to bottom") is planted to five different clones of Pinot Noir; and Rockyfeller Vineyard on the Golden Mile in the southern Okanagan supplies the winery with its late-ripening red varieties, Cabernet Sauvignon, Merlot, Malbec and Shiraz. A new 6-hectare vineyard, called Freedom 75, sits directly below the winery. Planted with Chardonnay and Riesling clones, it will begin producing in 2013.

Jeff's portfolio is equally strong in both red and white wines, and not surprisingly, he makes a Shiraz. For a winery that produces 9,000 cases, the product list covers 18 labels, including another Aussie favourite, Liqueur Muscat.

Jackson-Triggs Okanagan Estate

The 42-hectare SunRock Vineyard, Jackson-Triggs Okanagan Estate's pride and glory, sits some 60 metres above Osoyoos Lake on a mountain slope at the southern end of the Okanagan Valley, in Canada's only pocket desert. With its sandy loam soil, the vineyard is densely planted at 3,360 vines per hectare. The extreme temperature changes between day and night produce ripe fruit with balancing acidity. This is red wine country, where Shiraz, Cabernet Sauvignon and Merlot thrive.

**Jackson-Triggs
Okanagan Estate**
38691–97th Street (off Highway 97)
Oliver, BC V0H 1T0
(866) 445-0559
(250) 498-4500
JacksonTriggsWinery.com

JoieFarm

Michael Dinn and winemaker Robert Thielicke take a well-deserved break.

JoieFarm
2825 Naramata Road
Naramata, BC V0H 1N0
(866) 422-5643
(250) 496-0073
joiefarm.com

I N A MERE eight years, JoieFarm has established itself as one of the leading small wineries in British Columbia. For three vintages between 2004 and 2006, it was a virtual winery — making its fascinating portfolio of Alsace-inspired wines at Penticton's Pentâge Winery. In the spring of 2007, proprietors Heidi Noble and husband Michael Dinn moved into their own small winery and planted an old orchard with the aromatic varieties Muscato Giallo and Gewürztraminer. They built a modern industrial 510-square-metre winery facility, naming their 2-hectare farm Joie (French for "joy") to express the pleasure that wine and food have brought to their lives personally and professionally. Heidi trained at the Stratford Chefs School in Ontario, and both she and Michael are trained sommeliers who have worked in several of Canada's top restaurants. Their enterprise started as a guest house and

JoieFarm owners Michael Dinn and Heidi Noble happily toast their good fortune.

an outdoor cooking school, where the lessons took place in the orchard — the story of which Heidi immortalized in her award-winning book *Menus from an Orchard Table*.

Running counter to the accepted wisdom in their choice of varieties for the Naramata Bench, the couple opted to concentrate on Alsace-style wines as suitable for the climate of the Okanagan and, according to Michael, an expression of "their affinity to the Asian-influenced West Coast cuisine of Vancouver and our own personal enjoyment in drinking Alsatian wines." While JoieFarm concentrated on white varieties in the early years, it has latterly expanded its portfolio to include rosé and Pinot Noir — they make one of the few Passe-Tout-Grains in Canada, a blend of Gamay and Pinot Noir. A new vineyard in Naramata has recently been planted to Pinot Noir and Chardonnay, which will become the mother block for the winery's Reserve Series label, called En Famille. Heidi, along with Robert Thielicke, formerly with Mount Boucherie, is responsible for the winemaking, while Michael oversees sales and marketing.

Laughing Stock Vineyards

Laughing Stock is a double pun relating to David and Cynthia Enns's financial background. In 2003, the couple gave up trading financial stocks in Vancouver for growing vine stocks on what is now an 11-hectare site on the Naramata Bench. The financial premise is carried over to their labels (which mimic stock quotes) and to the name of their signature Bordeaux-style red — Portfolio. Laughing Stock's other red and white blends are labelled Blind Trust. The gravity-flow winery, with its barrel cellar, was built into the hillside and opened in 2005.

Laughing Stock Vineyards
1548 Naramata Road
Penticton, BC V2A 8T7
(250) 493-VINO (8466)
laughingstock.ca

David Enns, proprietor and winemaker.

Mission Hill Family Estate Winery

John Simes, Mission Hill's award-winning winemaker.

Mission Hill Family Estate Winery
1730 Mission Hill Road
West Kelowna, BC V4T 2E4
(250) 768-7611
(250) 768-6448
missionhillwinery.com

I F DIONYSUS, THE god of wine, dreamed of a cathedral in which to celebrate the fermented grape, he could happily take residence here at Mission Hill. Perched high above Okanagan Lake on Mount Boucherie, the property commands a magnificent view over the surrounding area — especially from its Terrace Restaurant. When Anthony von Mandl purchased the rundown facility in 1981, he dreamed of making it a beacon to the world for the wines of British Columbia. To achieve that end, he unashamedly patterned it after the late Robert Mondavi's creation in California's Napa Valley. The style of the original Mission Hill, with its 18th-century antiques, tiled floors and whitewashed walls, was reminiscent of the Mondavi model, as was Anthony's penchant for associating his enterprise with cultural events, including support for the Vancouver Symphony Orchestra.

In 1992, as part of his strategy to improve the quality of the wines, Anthony hired New Zealander John Simes, then chief winemaker at Montana Wines. John rewarded his boss's gamble by winning the 1994 Avery Trophy at the International Wine and Spirit Competition in London for the Best

Okanagan Valley

Chardonnay in the World. It was his first effort—Mission Hill Grand Reserve Chardonnay 1992. With the winemaking in good hands, Anthony began to turn his sights to the winery itself.

Anthony owns a beverage-alcohol importing company called Mark Anthony Brands, and the success of its sales of Corona beer and Mike's Hard Lemonade in Canada helped finance a complete makeover of the Mission Hill winery. He showed his confidence in the future of the B.C. wine industry by investing $35 million in rebuilding the winery and purchasing new vineyards.

The result is astonishing. The completely renovated property, with its collection of ancient glassware, a Leger carpet and a Chagall-inspired wall hanging, is one the most extraordinary wine facilities I have seen anywhere on my wine travels. The most dramatic feature, which can be seen and heard for miles around, is the slender 12-storey bell tower whose four bells, commissioned by Anthony and cast in France, chime every quarter of the hour—much to the chagrin of some of his neighbours. The largest bell weighs nearly 800 kilograms. The manufacturers, Fonderie Paccard in Annecy, also cast the bells for St. Patrick's Cathedral in New York City and Sacré-Cœur in Paris. The bells pealed for the

first time on December 11, 2000 — the day Mission Hill picked its Chardonnay Icewine 2000.

To enter the winery, visitors walk under a large concrete arch (similar to the hacienda style of Mondavi's façade) that frames the tower and the winery buildings. The feeling evoked is not dissimilar to entering a Greek temple, with its solitude and sense of calm, the elegant proportions of the buildings and the open green spaces.

Anthony hired Seattle architect Tom Kundig to transform the Mission Hill winery. Kundig remembers first visiting the site and being overwhelmed by its natural beauty, recognizing intuitively that anything he did would be secondary to the landscape itself. The results are one of the architectural wonders of the wine world. Equally dramatic below ground as it is above, Mission Hill boasts a magnificent crypt-like barrel-aging cellar that extends in a gigantic L-shape under the winery. It had to be blasted out of the rock face, much of which has been left exposed, creating a subtle contrast to the smoothness of the concrete arches and buttresses. A visitor can look down on the cellar through an "oculus" — a large piece of glass set in a well outside that directs the only natural light to the cellar below. And Oculus is the name Anthony von Mandl gave to his flagship red wine, a Bordeaux blend of Cabernet Sauvignon, Merlot and Cabernet Franc.

Anthony began buying vineyard land in 1995 and since then has acquired close to 400 hectares in 25 plots. To assist him, winemaker John Simes is able to call upon the consulting expertise of the legendary flying winemaker Michel Rolland of France and Riesling specialist Fritz Hasselbach of Weingut Gunderloch in Germany's Rheinhessen region.

Nk'Mip Cellars

Nk'Mip Cellars
400 Rancher Creek Road
Osoyoos, BC V0H 1V0
(250) 495-2985
nkmipcellars.com

A JOINT-VENTURE PROJECT FOUNDED in 2000 with Vincor, Nk'Mip Cellars is North America's first aboriginal-owned and -operated winery. The winery's name, pronounced *In-ka-meep*, comes from the local Salish dialect and means "place where the river joins the lake," and visitors sense a distinct feeling of spirituality and reverence for place when they enter the property. The Osoyoos Band's viticulture history dates back to 1968, when members first planted the Imkameep Vineyard. The 12,950-hectare reservation that is home to the band contains 25 percent of all vineyard land planted in the Okanagan Valley. Currently, the band farms 142 hectares of grapes.

Nk'Mip Cellars' attractive labels feature the company logo — a pictograph of a turtle, a symbol of wisdom and vision, painted on an arrowhead, which is in turn a symbol of the power and heritage of the vineyard. The winery, designed in Santa Fe style, is located in Canada's only pocket desert, where temperatures can reach 41°C. Sitting on an arid bench with a dramatic backdrop of rattlesnake-infested granite hills, the facility overlooks Osoyoos Lake, not far from the Washington state border. Across the lake, you can see Vincor's Osoyoos Larose vineyards.

Adjacent to the winery is a desert interpretive and heritage

Aaron Crey, cellar supervisor, in the barrel room, above. At right, Nk'Mip's Santa Fe-style resort and winery buildings make a dramatic statement in the desert environment.

centre, built to educate visitors about the need to protect the remaining desert landscape and endangered species. A popular attraction for visitors is the snakepit, where the curious can get a first-hand view of the metre-long rattlers that are captured, marked with electronic tracing chips and returned to the wild, where they can be tracked and their habits studied. The boardwalk paths are festooned with snake warning signs.

Incorporated into the band's ambitious business model for the winery are a series of ventures that draw tourists to this remote area: Nk'Mip Resort incorporates the Spirit Ridge Vineyard Resort & Spa, the Nk'Mip Conference Centre, the Solstice Spa and the Mica Restaurant at Spirit Ridge, as well as the Desert Cultural Centre, the nine-hole, par-35 Sonora Dunes Golf Course and the Nk'Mip RV Park.

Once you've taken a look at the snakes in captivity at the nearby Desert Cultural Centre, there's a good chance you'll need a glass of wine. And while you might have a little difficulty pronouncing the names of some of winemaker Randy Picton's offerings — such as the Meritage red blend Qwam Qwmt Syrah or MeR'R'IYM (which means "marriage"), the high quality of the wine will put the challenge in perspective.

Okanagan Crush Pad

Okanagan Crush Pad
16576 Fosbery Road
Summerland, BC V0H 1Z0
(250) 494-4445
okanagancrushpad.com

THE FIRST OF its kind in Canada, this multi-faceted enter-prise was only established in 2011, but it has a place here because it has already proven itself as a testing ground for virtual wineries and emerging winemakers. Okanagan Crush Pad was created by Christine Coletta and her husband Steve Lornie. The winery, a 720-square-metre facility, is an ultra-modern concrete and glass building in Summer-land's 4-hectare Switchback Vineyard. Until 2005, this plot was an orchard, but it is now planted entirely to Pinot Gris. Okanagan Crush Pad's resident winemaker is Michael Bartier, formerly the magician at Road 13 Vineyards. Michael makes a variety of wines here under such labels as Haywire, Bartier & Scholefield, Bartier Bros., Bella Wines, Harper's Trail Estate Winery in Kamloops and Rafter F Winery. Tom DiBello, the long-time winemaker at CedarCreek who now consults with Harry McWatters at Vintage Consulting Group Inc., makes his DiBello Syrah, Merlot and Chardonnay at Okanagan Crush Pad.

Okanagan Crush Pad owners Christine Coletta and Steve Lornie with chief winemaker Michael Bartier.

In addition to making Michael Bartier's wine-making skills available to clients, Okanagan Crush Pad provides what they call "field to market" expertise — assisting in the marketing, label design and promotion of wines produced at the state-of-the-art facility, which has a 25,000-case capacity. The six 1,800-litre black concrete "egg" fermenters are a standout feature of this customized crushing facility, giving the pad a distinct space-age look.

Chris and Steve have big plans. The company has purchased 128 hectares of raw ranchland in Summerland's Garnet Valley, where they are planting Pinot Gris, Pinot Noir and Cabernet Franc on the advice of their Chilean terroir expert, Pedro Parra, and their Italian consulting winemaker, Alberto Antonini. Planting of the initial 24-hectare plots began in the spring of 2013. The vineyard will give See Ya Later's vineyard on Hawthorne Mountain a run for its money as the highest vineyard in the Okanagan Valley (though those laurels may very well go to Don and Elaine Triggs for their Margaret's Bench vineyard at Culmina Family Estate in Oliver, which tops off at 595 metres). According to the winery's general manager, Julian Scholefield, "We will be making an estimated 30,000 cases from the 2012 harvest, which is more than double what was made at Okanagan Crush Pad in 2011." In addition, the home label Haywire will be adding a Gamay and a sparkling wine to its portfolio.

Osoyoos Larose

Osoyoos Larose
38691 Highway 97 North
Oliver, BC V0H 1T0
(250) 498-4981
osoyooslarose.com

OSOYOOS LAROSE IS the only winery in Canada that makes only one wine — a blended red featuring the Bordeaux varieties Merlot, Cabernet Sauvignon and Cabernet Franc. The top selection goes into the Grand Vin and the rest into a less costly bottling under the Pétales d'Osoyoos label. This resolutely Bordelais model came about as a result of a joint-venture project between Vincor and the giant Bordeaux shipper Groupe Taillan, which the two partners launched in 1999. Together, they envisioned creating a wine of "global stature" in the southern Okanagan Valley. To this end, they planted a 24-hectare vineyard with all five Bordeaux red varieties. The first vintage was 2001, and they called the wine Osoyoos Larose, a marriage of the vineyard location in Osoyoos and Château Gruaud-Larose, the flagship of six Bordeaux properties owned by Groupe Taillan.

The vines, a combination of different rootstocks and clones, were prepared at the Mercier nursery in Bordeaux and shipped over to Canada to be planted by hand. The trellising system was selected to allow for superior canopy management and to promote good air movement and maximum sun exposure. Planting the vines much closer together than is typically done

Viticulturist Catherine Scott-Taggart assesses the grapes in the manicured Osoyoos vineyard.

in Canada produced a lower yield and more concentrated fruit quality by virtue of the competition that results.

French oenologists Michel Rolland and Alain Sutre consulted on the project, and for the first 12 vintages, the wine was made by Pascal Madevon, a former winemaker from Château La Tour Blanche in St. Christoly du Médoc. In 2012, Pascal joined a new winery, Culmina Family Estate, owned by Elaine and Don Triggs. (At the time of writing, Constellation Brands was conducting a search in France for Pascal's replacement as winemaker.) It was Don Triggs, as chair and CEO of Jackson-Triggs, who initiated the original project. Originally, the wine was made in the Jackson-Triggs' facility in Oliver as a winery within a winery, but Vincor subsequently built a stand-alone winery for the brand.

Painted Rock Estate Winery

Gabriel Reis, cellar master.

Painted Rock Estate Winery
400 Smythe Drive
Penticton, BC V2A 8W6
(250) 493-6809
paintedrock.ca

Painted Rock takes its name from the ancient pictographs painted on the rocky bluffs that rise behind the 24.3-hectare benchland property overlooking the eastern shore of Penticton's Skaha Lake. These 500-year-old paintings by First Nations artists had a special resonance for John Skinner, who had stumbled upon a 1972 article describing his father, a Canadian Forces fighter pilot and an amateur archaeologist , digging for Indian artifacts in Vancouver Island's Comox Valley. After discovering the rock paintings, John consulted the local First Nations band for an interpretation. When he learned that the pictographs represented "a spirit walk" or a "coming of age," John knew that their message coincided perfectly with his vision for his new enterprise. It was also a perfect way for him to honour the memory of his late father.

John, a former investment broker, purchased the property in 2004. He and his wife Trish had dreamed of owning

their own vineyard ever since a trip to the south of France when they had toured the region's wineries. The land was originally an apricot farm — at one time, it represented the largest planting of apricots in the British Empire — but following a devastating infestation of gypsy moths, it had lain fallow for some 17 years. The couple contoured the land for vineyards and a year later planted 10 hectares of Bordeaux varieties — Cabernet Sauvignon, Cabernet Franc, Merlot, Malbec and, their favourite, Petit Verdot — as well as Syrah and some Chardonnay.

Painted Rock's first vintage was 2007, and the winery has quickly gained cult status, particularly for its flagship blend, Red Icon — this despite the fact that the winery's tasting room, at roughly the size of a galley kitchen, must be the world's smallest. Michael Bartier of Okanagan Crush Pad consults to the winery, as does the Bordeaux-based oenologist Alain Sutre.

Poplar Grove Winery

Stefan Arnasen, winemaker, and Ian Sutherland, executive winemaker.

Poplar Grove Winery
425 Middle Bench Road
Penticton, BC V2A 8T6
(250) 493-9463
poplargrove.ca

O N CANADA DAY 2011, Poplar Grove owners Tony Holler, Ian Sutherland and Bernard Sali presided over the opening of a beautifully designed 880-square-metre cedar-clad winery situated on the southwestern slope of Munson Mountain. Facing the city of Penticton, the building's wall-to-wall panoramic windows command one of the area's best views of the Naramata Bench and Lake Okanagan. The winery is also home to The Vanilla Pod, a fine restaurant that has already established itself as a destination for food enthusiasts. The restaurant terrace looks out over a 1-hectare vineyard planted to Cabernet Franc and Pinot — the two varietals that Ian Sutherland believes the region should make its own.

This high-tech, contemporary operation is a far cry from the garagiste winery that Ian founded with his then-wife Gitta in

1993. Together, they had purchased a 4-hectare apple orchard, removed the trees and planted a vineyard to Merlot and Cabernet Franc. To save on overhead, the modest winery operation shared space with a cheese-making company. In 2007, Tony Holler, a pharmaceutical executive, bought into Poplar Grove and became the major shareholder. Tony brought to the partnership 44.5 hectares of vineyards in the southern Okanagan, which ceded Ian total control over the fruit for the estate wines he made with winemakers Stefan Arnasen and Nadine Allander.

In addition, Tony had purchased the site on Munson Mountain that would become the new home for Poplar Grove. That investment allowed the company to expand its portfolio and introduce a second tier of value-priced wines under the Monster Wines label. Since then, the company has acquired another site at the corner of Tupper Road and Middle Bench Road, just down the hill from the current winery, where they plan to build a winery and tasting room dedicated to Monster Wines.

Quails' Gate Estate Winery

Quails' Gate Estate Winery
3303 Boucherie Road
West Kelowna, BC V1Z 2H3
(800) 420-9463 (WINE)
(250) 769-4451
quailsgate.com

IN 1956, RICHARD Stewart purchased property on the slopes of the Boucherie Mountain Bench; five years later, he planted a vineyard. The original vines were Chasselas, planted in error, his grandson Tony confesses, adding that, "though none of these original plantings exist, we do still grow Chasselas as one of our most popular wines." In 1989, Richard's son Ben Stewart and his wife Ruth established a family enterprise with Quails' Gate Estate Winery. The Stewart family has long had a particular fondness for the Pinot Noir grape; in fact, they claim to have been the first in Canada to plant a commercial vineyard of the French Dijon clone of Pinot Noir. In homage, the winery now produces extremely limited lots of a series of Dijon clone Pinots.

Quails' Gate seems to have a tradition of hiring "down under" winemakers, beginning with Jeff Martin, who now owns La Frenz in Naramata. Jeff created the winery's bold Burgundian

Once dotted with orchards, the slopes bordering Okanagan Lake are prime lands for viticulture, thanks to the moderating effect of the lake.

style of Pinot Noir and Chardonnay and the curiosity, Old Vine Foch—a hybrid variety dismissed by most growers but exotic in the hands of Quails' Gate's winemakers. Jeff was followed by another Australian, Peter Draper, who, tragically, died at the young age of 39 in 1999. Ashley Hooper, a third Aussie, took over for three years before returning home. The current winemaker, Grant Stanley, trained in New Zealand at Ata Rangi.

A 2005 renovation and expansion of the winery's exceptional restaurant, Old Vines Restaurant & Wine Bar, transformed it into an all-season destination. The restaurant looks out at Quails' Gate's 32 hectares of immaculately manicured vineyards, which sweep down almost to the edge of Lake Okanagan and run up to the encroaching housing developments on the hills above.

Ben Stewart has halted the march of construction with a dense planting of Pinot Noir, Chardonnay, Merlot and Cabernet Sauvignon. Today, Quails' Gate, which owns 8 hectares next to Osoyoos Larose in the southern Okanagan, farms 73 vineyard hectares in the valley. The estate currently produces a very small offering of Pinot Gris from the Three Wolves Vineyard, which is farmed by the Drought family on the Boucherie slopes.

Red Rooster Winery

"Entertain them and they will come" would be a good description of what happens at Red Rooster — the little winery that grew. The cathedral-like winery facility, with its green lawns, a vast "wishing fountain" and a patio around the wine shop offering welcome shade, has become a tourist destination. Also much appreciated by visitors is the controversial sculpture titled *The Baggage Handler* by local artist Michael Hermesh. The 2-metre-tall piece, which depicts a naked man (nicknamed "Frank") with a suitcase in his hand, caused an uproar when it was displayed at Penticton's Marina Way traffic roundabout in February 2005. Seven months later, the winery was purchased by Andrés.

Red Rooster Winery
891 Naramata Road
Penticton, BC V2A 8T5
(250) 492-2424
redroosterwinery.com

Road 13 Vineyards

Québec-born winemaker Jean-Martin Bouchard.

Road 13 Vineyards
799 Ponderosa Road, Road 13
Oliver, BC V0H 1T1
(250) 498-8330
road13vineyards.com

ROAD 13 HAS a colourful history. The Okanagan Valley property was originally owned by three Russian field engineers who were expelled by the communists after the 1917 Russian Revolution. Taking advantage of the water made available by irrigation canals built by the province, the engineers planted fruit trees and ground crops. After a series of owners, the site was eventually purchased in 1980 by Peter Serwo, a former builder who constructed a medieval castle to house his winery and tasting room. The castle, positioned in the middle of the 8-hectare vineyard Peter planted in 1982, was complete with battlements, a drawbridge, a conical copper dome — and a suit of armour that guarded one of its towers. Named Golden Mile Cellars, the winery was sold to Mick and Pam Luckhurst in 2003. Mick, who was in construction, was no doubt impressed by Peter's chutzpah in building a castle in the desert, while Pam was a banker who had been wooed into the industry by the romance of wine.

Their first winemaker was the California-trained Lawrence Herder, who now operates the Herder Winery in the Similkameen Valley. He was followed by Michael Bartier, who is now in charge of Okanagan Crush Pad. In 2008, the Luckhursts changed the name of the winery to Road 13. Increasing their vineyard holdings to 18 hectares, they've upped production to 25,000 cases as Road 13 from Golden Mile's 1,000 cases. In a nod to the property's storied history, they named their three vineyards Home, Castle and Peter's. Each of the winery's blends and varietal wines bears the company logo on the label — a tractor, which speaks to Mick's fondness for farm equipment. In fact, he has a collection of five working tractors plus two that decorate the front entrance to the property.

Road 13's wines are now made by Jean-Martin Bouchard, who was the original winemaker at Ontario's Hidden Bench until 2010. Pam and Mick release Road 13 wines under three distinct labels: Honest John's — a red blend, a rosé and a white blend; Road 13 white and red varietals; and Jackpot — premium white and red small-lot varietals and blends.

Okanagan Valley

Sandhill Wines

Sandhill, part of Calona Vineyards owned by Andrés, is a unique boutique operation in that its winemaker, Howard Soon, produces only single vineyard wines. Howard sources his fruit from six diverse vineyard properties, three of which are located on Black Sage Road in the southern Okanagan — Sandhill Estate, Osprey Ridge and Phantom Creek (named by a Canadian wine magazine as one of the "Top Ten vineyards around the world"). The other three are King Family, north of Penticton; Hidden Terrace, north of Oliver; and Vanessa Vineyard in the Similkameen Valley. Sandhill's best products are marketed under their Small Lots program.

Sandhill Wines
1125 Richter Street
Kelowna, BC V1Y 2K6
(888) 246-4472
(250) 762-9144
sandhillwines.ca

See Ya Later Ranch

See Ya Later's vineyards, 41 hectares in all, are carved out of rock and forest at one of the highest elevations in the province. Wine grapes have been grown here since the early 1960s. Formerly Le Comte winery, the property was purchased in 1995 by Harry McWatters, who changed the name to Hawthorne Mountain. Known as See Ya Later Ranch since 2003, this is the only winery in the world I know of that features a dog cemetery. Several of the faithful companions of the original owner, Major Hugh Fraser, are buried here, now memorialized by the angel-winged dogs on the series of See Ya Later labels.

See Ya Later Ranch
2575 Green Lake Road
Okanagan Falls, BC V0H 1R0
(250) 497-8267
sylranch.com

Summerhill Pyramid Winery

Winemaker Eric von Krosigk, a B.C. native, developed his craft in Germany.

Summerhill Pyramid Winery
4870 Chute Lake Road
Kelowna, BC V1W 4M3
(800) 667-3538
(250) 764-8000
summerhill.bc.ca

STEPHEN CIPES, the owner of Summerland Pyramid Winery, is part philosopher, part showman. A committed environmentalist, he built the first organic winery in British Columbia and the first to have a certified biodynamic vineyard. "Where grapes enjoy their lives is also the place where humans enjoy their lives," he says. "Grapes like to have the movement of air and good water, and having good water is what we humans like too. Ideal weather is where it's dry. Wherever grapes are happy is where humans are happy."

An expatriate New York real estate developer who escaped the city 20 years ago to forge a healthier lifestyle, Stephen's flair for the dramatic is evident in the huge sparkling wine bottle that appears to float above a giant champagne flute on the winery terrace. Suspended in the air, the bottle pours its bubbling wine but never empties — an apt metaphor, perhaps, for Stephen's own enthusiasm and energy, especially when it comes to his winery.

Set behind and slightly above the winery is a four-storey-high, 302-square-metre replica of Cheops, the great pyramid at El Giza, Egypt. The structure, at a little less than a tenth the size of the original, is the most recognized icon in the Okanagan and the second such pyramid to be built at Summerhill. Its presence represents an ongoing scientific experiment — the winery's sparkling wines are aged here — which Stephen has heralded as an overwhelming success. "There is," he has written, "a definite and profound effect on liquids placed in the sacred geometry."

On the terrace overlooking the vineyard and the lake is the winery's Peace Park, a half-submerged globe surrounded by flowers and a message on a pole that reads, in 16 languages, "May Peace Prevail on Earth."

All of these imaginative elements make Summerhill's claim to be the most visited winery in British Columbia more than plausible. According to Stephen, 300,000 wine-loving tourists visit Summerhill Pyramid Winery every year.

In 2003, Stephen, true to his spiritual leanings, introduced a series of organic wines under the Enchanted Vine label. A back label for the sparkling wine dosed with Icewine, Inspiration Methode Traditionelle 1997, reads:

"Blessed by Shaman Chelsea Wise, Inspiration is the elixir for nurturing our creativity. It is the rising of our passion to meet the balance of our wisdom. Inspiration has been infused with the power to unfold the seed of our potential."

Winemaker Eric von Krosigk, who helped found the winery in 1991, has been instrumental in several start-up operations since then. A sparkling-wine specialist, he returned to Summerhill as head winemaker in 2006. Eric is one of the most awarded winemakers in the history of the B.C. wine industry.

Sumac Ridge Estate Winery

What's not to love about a winery that began life as a nine-hole golf course? Founders Harry McWatters and vineyardist Lloyd Schmidt purchased the golf course on Highway 97, just north of Summerland, in 1981, planting 2 hectares of Riesling and Gewürztraminer. The winery, the oldest estate winery in the province, put out its first vintage in 1987 and has pioneered the production of sparkling wine in British Columbia with their Steller's Jay brand. Today, the winery, now owned by Constellation Brands, farms 20 hectares on Black Sage Road as well as the original vines adjacent to the winery.

Sumac Ridge Estate Winery
17403 Highway 97 North
Summerland, BC V0H 1Z0
(250) 494-0451
sumacridge.com

Harry McWatters
Meet the Godfather

TO CALL HARRY MCWATTERS the Godfather of B.C. Wines might evoke a frown or a few salty words from the man who has been at the centre of the province's wine industry for more than 40 years. Not that Harry would object to being called a Godfather, but he does have a thing about people calling British Columbia B.C.

Harry's career in wine began in 1968 in the sales department of the now defunct Penticton-based winery Casabello. Ten years later, he was promoted to director of marketing. In 1980, he founded Sumac Ridge, the first estate winery in British Columbia and the only winery in Canada at that time to have its own nine-hole golf course. A born promoter and salesman, Harry convinced a group of wineries and local businessmen in the Okanagan Valley to establish the Okanagan Wine Festival Society and acted as its founding president. In 1990, he was appointed by the Province of British Columbia to chair the newly formed British Columbia Wine Institute, a position that he held for five years and for which he served as a director for 17 years. As if his workload were not heavy enough, Harry bought the old Le Comte winery in 1995 and changed its name to Hawthorne Mountain. The winery would undergo another name change to See Ya Later Ranch when Vincor purchased both of Harry's wineries in the spring of 2000. Harry continued on as president of both, even as he assumed responsibilities as a Vincor vice-president. He

retired in 2008, only to then establish the Vintage Consulting Group Inc. and the Okanagan Wine Academy.

In June 2001, Harry was presented with an Honorary Doctor of Laws Degree from Okanagan University College in recognition of the pivotal role he has played in the development of both British Columbia's and Canada's wine industry. In 2007, the City of Penticton named him as one of the 20 Most Influential People of the Century.

Tantalus Vineyards

Tantalus Vineyards
1670 Dehart Road
Kelowna, BC V1W 4N6
(877) 764-0078
(250) 764-0078
tantalus.ca

Warwick Shaw, vineyard manager, and David Paterson, winemaker.

IN ADDITION TO being the name of a mythical king of Phrygia, who was punished for revealing the secrets of the gods, "tantalus" is the term for a stand of decanters, usually three, none of which can be withdrawn until the grooved bar that secures their stoppers is released. Perhaps not the best mental image for a winery that wants to sell its products, but then, these wines are worthy of keeping under lock and key. Tantalus made its reputation with Riesling produced from some of the oldest vines in the valley.

The Dulik family has farmed this property on the eastern slopes of the Okanagan Valley, overlooking Lake Okanagan and the city of Kelowna, for 60 years. The site, originally called Pioneer Vineyards, was first planted to grapes in 1927, which makes it one of the oldest continuously producing vineyards in the province. Den Dulik planted Riesling as early as 1978. In 1997, his daughter Susan opened a small winery on the

vineyard site, planning to focus on the Pinot family of grapes. She called it Pinot Reach Cellars, but her winemaker, Roger Wong, made such a string of award-winning Rieslings that this grape became their signature wine.

In 2004, the winery was sold to Eric Savics, a Vancouver stockbroker, and Eira Thomas, a geologist. Eric became sole owner the following year. Under new ownership, the winery's name was changed to Tantalus Vineyards. The facility was immediately upgraded and expanded with new equipment and cooperage, and grape varieties not suited to the vineyard's conditions were rooted out. Tantalus opened its streamlined new LEED-built (Leadership in Energy and Environmental Design—a North American standard for rating the sustainability of commercial and industrial buildings) winery in 2010, the first to be certified in British Columbia. Winemaker David Paterson, who received his winemaking degree from Lincoln University in New Zealand and has worked vintages in Oregon, New Zealand, Australia and Burgundy, gets his Riesling, Pinot Noir and Chardonnay grapes exclusively from the 30-hectare vineyard that slopes down to Lake Okanagan. Among the 4,000-case production is an interesting oddity for the Okanagan—an Icewine made from Syrah. The winery's attractive labels feature a series of masks by West Coast First Nations carver Dempsey Bob. And at the age of 75, incidentally, former owner Den Dulik still works every day in the winery.

Tinhorn Creek Vineyards

Tinhorn Creek Vineyards
537 Tinhorn Creek Road
Box 2010
Oliver, BC V0H 1T0
(888) 484-6467
(250) 498-3743
tinhorn.com

AMERICAN SANDRA OLDFIELD studied at California's celebrated wine school, UC Davis, where she met her husband Kenn. The California connection in turn inspired the style of winery the Oldfields created with Bob and Brenda Shaunessy in 1993. Sandra Oldfield will tell you that they modelled Tinhorn Creek after Napa Valley's Newton Vineyard on Spring Mountain. Like Newton, this modernistic, mustard-yellow building is set majestically on a hillside — in this case, above Oliver's Golden Mile — its entrance embellished by a rock garden and a soothing water fountain. Inside, visitors can watch the winemaking process from interior galleries overlooking the stainless steel tanks, oak barrels and the cellar below.

The winery takes its name from the creek that runs through the property. In 1895, a gold-mining concern called the Tinhorn Quartz Mining Company was registered here. Today, however,

the only gold struck on the property are the medals Oldfield's wines win in national and international competitions. Ever since Tinhorn Creek's 1998 Merlot won Red Wine of Year at the Canadian Wine Awards, this variety has been Oldfield's signature wine, garnering medals in every competition in which it has been entered. The fruit comes from the 52.6-hectare Diamondback Vineyard on Black Sage Road, a property that oil executive Bob Shaunessy bought in 1993. That same year, he also purchased the 12-hectare vineyard on the Golden Mile as the site for the winery. As quality-driven as Tinhorn Creek's Merlot remains, it is Cabernet Franc that is now garnering the laurels. "Cabernet Franc loves the

Sandra Oldfield, Tinhorn Creek's winemaker and CEO, opposite, is an entrepreneur with both vision and determination.

heat, it loves the cold," says Sandra. "It has no problems with the winters; we see no damage in cold weather."

In 2004, the Oldfields and their staff planted more than 600 native shrubs, wildflowers and bunchgrass on one part of the property to restore the area to an antelope-brush plant community and create a natural habitat for B.C.'s endangered wildlife species.

Managed by Kenn Oldfield, this winery is one of the best-run operations in the valley. It's also home to one of the best restaurants in the Okanagan, the Miradoro.

Le Vieux Pin

Winemaker Severine Pinte.

Le Vieux Pin
5496 Black Sage Road
Oliver, BC V0H 1T0
(250) 498-8388
LeVieuxPin.ca

L E VIEUX PIN and its sister winery La Stella are owned by a company called Enotecca Winery and Resorts, founded by an Iranian couple, Sean and Saeedeh Salem, and financier Greg Thomas. Le Vieux Pin is resolutely French in its style and approach to wine and winemaking, La Stella uncompromisingly Italian. And yet one winemaker makes the wines for both labels. French-trained Severine Pinte is a passionate evangelist for Syrah and Viognier, the two varieties that compose the lion's share of the 3.2-hectare estate vineyard at Le Vieux Pin, along with the white Rhône grapes, Roussanne and Marsanne. Severine's winemaking philosophy is summed up in the words of the late Jean Hugel of the famed Alsace house: "One hundred percent of the quality of a true wine is already in the grapes, not in the cellars, where you can only lose quality."

An ancient pine tree that graces the northwest corner of the vineyard at Le Vieux Pin is the inspiration for the winery's name, and the facility's architectural look continues the French influence. The building looks much like a railway station in the French countryside, and its likeness appears as the winery's logo on all labels. Enotecca owns several small vineyard parcels in the south Okanagan, totalling 23.5 hectares in all, and these vineyards provide the fruit for both Le Vieux Pin and the Tuscan style of La Stella.

Le Vieux Pin's handwritten labels, front and back, offer the wine lover a host of information as to the soil in which the grapes were grown, the age of the vines, the harvest dates, the yield, the aging and the number of cases produced. The top-tier wines are called the Equinoxe Series. "These are wines," Rasoul Salehi, the company's general manager, says, "that capture the essence of south Okanagan in terms of showcasing the terroir — equal heat of the day, equal cool of the night, equal New World, equal Old World." The winery's second label is Petit Le Vieux Pin, which produces Sigma Rouge, Sigma Blanc and Sigma Rosé. From the hot 2009 vintage, Severine made the winery's first Cabernet-Syrah blend. Released in 2012 under the name Retouche, it pays homage to the 19th-century French practice of beefing up Bordeaux and Burgundy with Syrah from the Rhône.

Wild Goose Vineyards

Brothers Roland and Hagen Kruger (the winemaker) continue the work their father Adolf started in 1990 when he received British Columbia's second farm-gate winery licence. The family had to clear the slopes of brush and rocks to plant their first vines in 1983. The original tasting room was a space in a basement, but that was replaced in 2012 by a bright, spanking new building. Somewhat off the beaten track, Wild Goose has a folksy, welcoming style: Children get fruit juice samples while their parents taste the wines. Worthy of note, Hagen makes exemplary white wines.

Wild Goose Vineyards
2145 Sun Valley Way
Okanagan Falls, BC V0H 1R2
(250) 497-8919
wildgoosewinery.com

Orofino Vineyards

Orofino Vineyards
2152 Barcelo Road
Cawston, BC V0X 1C2
(250) 499-0068
orofinovineyards.com

Located in the Similkameen Valley, Orofino is named for the mountain that overlooks the property. "Orofino" is a Spanish word that means "fine gold" and harks back to earlier mining days, but it may well portend the colour of the medals this small winery will win with its beautifully crafted wines. John Weber, a teacher from Swift Current, Saskatchewan — about as far as you can get from wine growing in Canada — and his wife Virginia, a nurse with a diploma in horticulture, hit the ground running when they opened the winery in 2005. The 2.2-hectare vineyard was already 12 years old when they acquired it, and those well-seasoned vines provided them with mature fruit for a wine portfolio that includes Riesling, Chardonnay, Pinot Gris, Pinot Noir, Merlot and a Bordeaux blend they call Beleza.

The facility's 215-square-metre building, with a breezeway that separates the winery from the tasting room, is in a class by itself: It is the only facility in the country constructed

John Weber, winemaker and proprietor, presents his October crop.

from straw bales. The 54-centimetre-thick high-density walls maintain a constant temperature inside, and they also provide sufficient insulation (RD-60) for the barrel cellar and tasting room against the heat of the Similkameen summers. "The bales allow our barrel building to remain at around 17°C when it is 30 plus outside," says John. In keeping with their environmental agenda, the Webers completed an ambitious solar power project in 2012 that will convert all power consumption in the public tasting building from traditional power sources to solar power.

Domaine de Chaberton Estate Winery

Domaine de Chaberton Estate Winery
1064 – 216th Street
Langley, BC V2Z 1R3
(888) 332-9463
(604) 530-1736
domainedechaberton.com

DOMAINE DE CHABERTON is the largest and the oldest winery in the Fraser Valley. In 1980, when Claude and Inge Violet decided to make British Columbia their home, they chose a raspberry farm south of Langley amid horse and dairy farms. Claude's father had once owned a winery in Tarragona, Spain, and a vineyard and orchard near Montpellier, in southern France, named Domaine de Chaberton. Claude and German-born Inge chose the Fraser Valley, rather than the Okanagan, because it was nearer their potential market in Vancouver. Their success was yet another example of rugged individualism triumphing over accepted wisdom: Everyone insisted it was impossible to grow grapes in the cool climate of the Fraser Valley. Wisely, the couple planted only white varieties such as the early-ripening Bacchus, Angevine, Madeleine Sylvaner and Seigerrebe, sourcing their reds from a grower on Black Sage Road in the southern Okanagan.

Christina Mynen, of Tourism Langley, accompanies winemaker Barbara Hall on a vineyard inspection.

After 25 years, the Violets decided to retire in 2005, selling the winery to Anthony Cheng and Eugene Kwan. Anthony is a business executive who lives in Hong Kong but has had business interests in Vancouver for 20 years. Eugene is a business executive and lawyer; born in Shanghai, he grew up in Vancouver.

A cluster of dazzling white buildings, the winery includes a popular French bistro and a cedar-panelled Quonset hut that houses the barrel room. Depending on the weather, you can dine indoors at the Bacchus Bistro or outdoors, within sight of the beautifully groomed vineyard. In 1991, the first year of production, Domaine de Chaberton produced 3,000 cases. Today, the winery controls 20 hectares of vineyards, making it the third-largest estate winery in British Columbia, and produces in excess of 50,000 cases a year. Its long-time winemaker is Dr. Elias Phiniotis, who has overseen 22 vintages at Domaine de Chaberton.

Township 7 Vineyards & Winery

Township 7 began as a small Fraser Valley winery in a horse barn in Langley. Here Corey Coleman and his wife Gwen made medal-winning wines from their 2-hectare vineyard, purchasing grapes from the southern Okanagan. In 2004, they opened a second winery, a no-frills facility with 3 hectares of vines on the Naramata Bench outside Penticton. They sold both properties to restaurateur Mike Raffan in 2006. Winemaker Bradley Cooper, formerly at See Ya Later Ranch, carries on the tradition of producing sparkling wine in Langley.

**Township 7
Vineyards & Winery**
South Langley/Fraser Valley
21152 – 16th Avenue
Langley, BC V2Z 1K3
(604) 532-1766

Naramata Bench
1450 McMillan Avenue
Penticton, BC V24 8T4
(250) 770-1743

township7.com

Gail Simpson and Deborah Funnell.

Church & State Wines

Brentwood Bay's Kim Pullen, opposite, in his elegantly designed facility.

Brentwood Bay Winery
1445 Benvenuto Avenue
Central Saanich, BC V8M 1J5
(250) 652-2671

Coyote Bowl Winery
4516 Ryegrass Road
Oliver, BC V0H 1T1
(250) 498-2700

churchandstatewines.com

S ITUATED ON VANCOUVER Island between Victoria Butterfly Gardens and Butchart Gardens on the Saanich Penin-sula, Church & State Wines is unashamedly geared to the tourist trade. Cruise-ship clientele roll up at the winery's Brentwood Bay location for tastings and cellar tours in the vast barnlike building, which boasts a car park large enough to accommodate a fleet of buses. The impres-sive 1,950-square-metre redwood structure houses the winery, a shopping area and a bistro. Three-quarters of the winery's grapes come from the Okanagan and Similkameen valleys. With Church & State's acquisition of property near Oliver, now the site of the Coyote Bowl Vineyard and its new boutique winery, the emphasis at Brentwood Bay is on sparkling wines.

In the spring of 2005, Victoria businessman Kim Pullen took over the then-struggling winery and bought an initial 5.6 hectares of land along Okanagan's Golden Mile to plant a vineyard. Determined to make quality products, he ordered the dumping of $2 million worth of substandard wine already in the vats on Vancouver Island and hired Californian Bill Dyer as his consulting winemaker. Bill, who made wine at Sterling

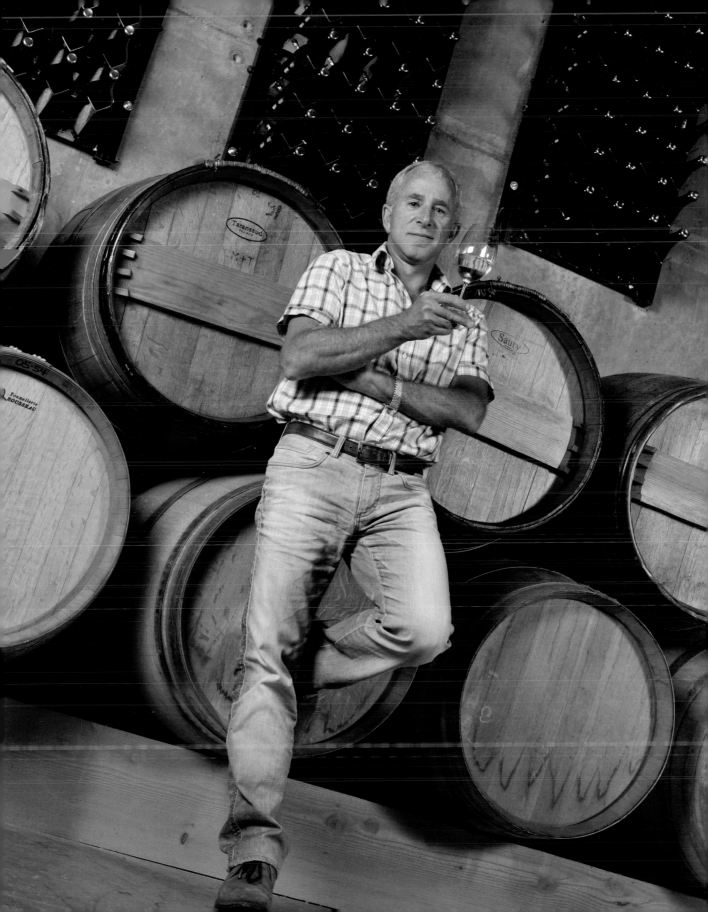

Vineyards in Napa and currently consults to Marimar Torres in Sonoma, was the man who created the stylish wines for Burrowing Owl when it opened. In 2009, Kim hired Canadian winemaker Jeff Del Nin, who had worked two vintages at Burrowing Owl and had extensive winemaking experience in Australia, where he discovered his passion for the Viognier grape. (Coincidentally, Kim had already planted this variety at the Coyote Bowl Vineyard.)

In 2011, Church & State opened an impressive tasting room in the vineyard. The tasting bar overlooks the barrel cellar, with floor-to-ceiling windows behind that look out onto the 44 hectares of vines now owned by the winery. The same year, Jeff added a Viognier and a white Rhône-style blend called Tre-Bella (Marsanne, Roussanne and Viognier) to his award-winning Syrah, bringing Church & State production to 13,000 cases.

Garry Oaks Winery

Owners Elaine Kozak and Marcel Mercier.

Garry Oaks Winery
1880 Fulford-Ganges Road
Salt Spring Island, BC V8K 2A5
(250) 653-4687
garryoakswinery.com

THE GARRY OAKS Winery may sound as if it were named after the owner, but in fact, it's named after a species of oak tree. *Quercus garryana*, also known as the Oregon White Oak, is unique to the Pacific Northwest region and can be found on Salt Spring Island, the largest of the Southern Gulf Islands. As a tribute to the tree, the winery's Classic Series of three wines carries the oak leaf as a logo on the label.

In 1999, Marcel Mercier, an environmental consultant, and Elaine Kozak, an economist, gave up the corporate world to purchase a 100-year-old fruit farm on Salt Spring. They created a 4-hectare terraced vineyard by carving out the steep, south-facing, sandy/gravelly loam slopes at the foot of Mount Maxwell, which overlooks the Burgoyne Valley. Today, the couple oversees the largest winery on the island, and their wines are 100 percent estate-grown.

The 280-square-metre winery, with its gabled roof and cedar siding, consists of a compound with two buildings. The main processing facility and the barrel room are connected by a courtyard. Set into a slope, one wall of the barrel room — which doubles as a tasting room — is half underground, and that helps to maintain an even cellar temperature throughout the year.

"Pinot Gris and Pinot Noir are our flagship wines," says Elaine, who makes the wines, while Marcel looks after the vineyard. "But we are very excited about the potential shown by Zweigelt, from which we make a varietal wine called Zeta. Zweigelt really likes our growing conditions, ripening ahead of the Pinots, and makes a deep-hued, spicy, fruit-forward wine that ages exceptionally well and with time develops a certain gravitas. We grow our grapes naturally; that is, we don't tent the vines [against the cold weather] like some vineyards on the coast do." Elaine also makes an unusual wine called Prism — a blend of Chardonnay and Gewürztraminer.

Venturi-Schulze Vineyards

Marilyn Schulze and Giordano Venturi.

Venturi-Schulze Vineyards
4235 Vineyard Road/
Trans-Canada Highway
Cobble Hill, BC V0R 1L0
(250) 743-5630
venturischulze.com

IN 1988, ITALIAN Giordano Venturi and Australian Marilyn Schulze purchased a 100-year-old farm in the Cowichan Valley on Vancouver Island, 45 minutes north of Victoria. Through dint of hard work, they have created a small, garagiste-style operation that has become something of a hidden treasure, given how difficult it is to acquire these wines.

The couple's perfectionism can be seen in the pristine condition of the vineyard, which is herbicide- and pesticide-free and is farmed without irrigation. "This is the island. We've got to roll with the punches," says Giordano. To combat the twin threats of inclement weather and birds, he tents the vines with plastic in early spring to protect against late frost and to ensure ripeness; in late summer, he nets the entire vineyard.

Venturi-Schulze wines are highly individual and intense; the lesser-known varieties are given proprietary brand names — Indigo for Schönburger; Sassi for Pinot Grigio and

Ortega; Nero Collina for Zweigelt and Dornfelder; and Brandenberg No. 3 for Madeleine Sylvaner. The owners raised a lot of eyebrows in 1996 when they bottled their entire portfolio of wines, including sparkling, under crown caps to avoid cork taint. Today, the industry is catching up to them by adopting screw caps, which Venturi-Schulze also now uses. In addition to the wines, Giordano, a native of Modena, makes a much sought-after balsamic vinegar.

Marilyn is as dedicated an evangelist for the wines of the island as her husband. "We want to drink wines with a sense of place," she says. "When we go to Alsace, we don't expect to drink Bordeaux, Burgundy or champagne. We expect to taste Alsace. So when people come to Vancouver Island, I would like everybody to know that they're having a taste of the island and be able to appreciate it as such."

Giordano and Marilyn live in a much-renovated and expanded 1893 farmhouse adjacent to the winery and the vinegar house, which is isolated, because vinegar stored near wine will turn the wine. In 2011, Venturi-Schulze opened a new tasting room, which was built with local woods and showcases the work of Cowichan Valley artisans.

This winery is on the must-visit list, but watch carefully for the sign. While Venturi-Schulze may be on the Trans-Canada Highway, it's hard to find. An appointment is imperative, as the proprietors "value their privacy and spend as much time as possible in the vineyard and winery."

Ontario

Ontario

The Cradle of Canada's Wine Industry

ONTARIO NOW HAS three designated wine-growing regions: Niagara Peninsula, Lake Erie North Shore and Prince Edward County. But more could be coming in the future — there are intrepid wine growers in Northumberland County and Georgian Bay (Coffin Ridge Boutique Winery and Georgian Hills Vineyards). And Prince Edward County may find itself competing with the Northumberland Hills. There is even a flourishing winery in Bruce County (Carrick Wines and Ciders), which shares the Niagara Escarpment with Canada's longest established wine-growing region, the Niagara Peninsula, and Burning Kiln in the south-coast region of Lake Erie North Shore.

Ontario is the largest wine region in Canada and the best known internationally. At the time of writing, 169 wineries were operating in the province (including fruit wineries), 132 of which produce Vintners Quality Alliance (VQA) wines (26 of these produce sparkling wines). The architecture of the facilities ranges from the traditional French château style (Château des Charmes, Peller Estates) to Ontario Gothic (Peninsula Ridge, Angels Gate) to contemporary modern (Jackson-Triggs, Stratus, Flat Rock, Fielding and Huff). There are also a couple of "virtual wineries" (Thomas Bachelder and Charles Baker, who don't have the bricks and mortar but make their wines under their own labels at Southbrook and Stratus, respectively).

So successful has the industry become that it has attracted the attention of the Burgundy shippers Boisset Family Estates, Michel Picard from La Maison Picard and Michel Laroche

Reif Estate Winery's Vidal Icewine, above. Situated along the northeastern shore of Pelee Island — now a destination for nature lovers and wine tourists — the Pelee Island Lighthouse, opposite, was originally built in 1833 and restored in 2000. The rich hues of a mid-October afternoon warm the vineyards of Angels Gate, previous spread.

from Domaine Laroche, as well as local and international entrepreneurs who are willing to invest millions of dollars to make Ontario wine. In June 2012, a group of Chinese investors bought Marynissen Estates, and in the same year, a Chinese businessman acquired Alvento Winery in Lincoln. You have only to tour the wineries in Niagara to see the extent of such investment in vineyard development, infrastructure and winemaking hardware.

The critical mass of wineries in the Niagara Peninsula has created a "Napa North" phenomenon. Fine restaurants, cooking classes, bike tours, concerts, theatre, jazz festivals and winery events have generated a tourism boom that sees busloads of local and foreign visitors flocking through winery tasting rooms. After seeing Niagara Falls, everyone, it seems, wants to discover Ontario wines. Lake Erie North Shore has suddenly blossomed with a host of new wineries, and this growing number will attract tourists to the southwest corner of the province. Ontario's newest region, Prince Edward County, already has the infrastructure in place — the restaurants, B&Bs, festivals and activities — to entice the wine traveller. It all adds up to one compelling idea: Ontario wine is glamorous, and the world has begun to take notice.

The cradle of the Canadian wine industry was not the Niagara Peninsula, where the greatest vineyard acreage is to be found, but a good 70 kilometres west in a town named Cooksville. Today it is called Mississauga, a city of 715,000 people just west of Toronto. It was here, on the banks of the Credit River, that a retired German soldier, Corporal Johann Schiller, settled on 8 hectares of land granted to him by the Crown for his military service in Canada in the early years of the 19th century.

There is some contention as to whether Schiller deserves the sobriquet as the Father of Canadian wine, but he certainly had winemaking experience in his native Rhineland. By 1811, he had domesticated the wild labrusca vines that grew along the banks of the Credit River and supplemented them with American hybrids furnished to him by settlers from Pennsylvania. Schiller made enough wine to satisfy his own needs and to sell to his neighbours.

While there is no documentary evidence about Schiller's winery enterprise over the years, an ambitious French aristocrat, Count Justin M. de Courtenay, resurrected Schiller's vineyard, doubling its size by planting Clinton and Isabella grapes. In 1864, he established the Vine Growers Association. De Courtenay's label, Clair House, became the largest brand in Ontario, and his wine was exhibited in Paris to celebrate Canada's nationhood in 1867. In the same year, a farmer in Queenston named Porter Adams was shipping grapes to the Toronto market for home winemakers, and John Kilborn, a farmer who owned 6.9 hectares on Ontario Street in Beamsville, was selling his wine locally for $1.75 a gallon (4 litres). With typical vintners' braggadocio, he wrote in the *Canadian Agriculturalist* that his wine "probably would bring in more if we asked for it. At all events it is worth four times as much as the miserable stuff sold by our merchants under the name of wine."

Winemaking in the late 19th century was more of a basement hobby than a business. When it was not sold through the kitchen door, it would have been available at the local drugstore. The problem for those early winemakers, whether they were making wine for their own consumption or for profit, was

the alcohol level. Native hybrids such as Isabella and Catawba are low in sugar but high in acidity, so sugar had to be added during fermentation to bring up the alcohol level.

THE FIRST GROWERS along the Niagara Peninsula planted their vines in large part to service the fresh fruit trade. One of the best table varieties — and a much-favoured taste in jams and jellies — was the Concord grape, whose flavour is familiar to us today in grape juice and virtually all grape-flavoured products. This hardy, unkillable grape was propagated by a Concord, Massachusetts, grower who rejoiced in the name of Ephraim Wales Bull and named the grape after the town he lived in.

The only problem with the Concord grape is that it makes awful wine. (Indeed, since 1988, it and its labrusca kin have been legally banned from Ontario table wines.) As grape juice, the Concord can be enjoyable, but when fermented, it concentrates a natural chemical compound called methyl anthranilate that gives the wine the unfortunate odour of an agitated fox. Yet Concord, because it was easy to grow and gave high yields, was to become the workhorse grape of the Ontario wine industry up until the 1940s. And as the major component in the "Duck" range of pop wines, the Concord grape provided 90 percent of company profits until the late 1970s. (In order to mask the foxy bouquet and flavour,

Canadian wineries indulged in the questionable practice of "stretch" — the addition of sugar, colouring agents and water. An imperial ton of grapes can yield about 160 gallons/727 litres of wine. Through stretching, the large commercial wineries were able to more than triple that.)

THE AMERICANS SENT not only their grapes north but their entrepreneurs too. In the 1860s, most of the winemaking operations in Ontario were small-volume enterprises, a sideline for farmers who had crops other than grapes to harvest. In 1866, "a company of gentlemen from Kentucky," according to a letter in the *Canadian Farmer*, "who have been in the grape business for 14 years, have purchased a farm on Pelee Island and planted 12 hectares this spring, and intend to plant 8 hectares next spring." They named their winery Vin Villa, the stone ruins of which can still be seen on the island. Vin Villa sold grapes and finished wine to an enterprising grocer in Brantford, Major J.S. Hamilton, whose store was granted a royal charter to sell wine and liquor in 1871. Eventually, Hamilton took over the Vin Villa, and the company that bore his name was sold in 1949 to London Winery (which was acquired by Vincor in 1996).

By 1890, there were 35 commercial wineries in Ontario, two-thirds of which were located in Essex County, in the southwest of the province. The pre-eminence of Essex as Canada's grape-growing centre lasted for 30 years. By 1921, however, the grapevines — close to 810 hectares — had been torn out and replaced by more profitable cash crops, such as tobacco and soft fruit. A mere 20 hectares of vines remained, but this concentration was still greater than anywhere else in Canada.

IN 1873, GEORGE BARNES started a winery in St. Catharines on the banks of the old Welland Canal. There was no mistaking the company's purpose in the name on the wine label: Ontario Grape Growing and Wine Manufacturing Company, Limited. What this moniker lacked in imagination, it compensated for in longevity. The company operated as Barnes Wines until 1988, when Château-Gai purchased it.

George Barnes' vines had been in the ground for a year when Thomas Bright and his partner, F.A. Shirriff, opened a winery in Toronto. In naming it the Niagara Falls Wine Company, the pair must have instinctively realized they would have to move nearer their grape supply — and in 1890, move they did to the outskirts of that border town. In 1911, the company changed its name to T.G. Bright and Company. More than 80 years later, Cartier and Inniskillin would merge with T.G. Bright to form Vincor, Canada's largest winery group.

THE CLOSING YEARS of the 19th century showed remarkable growth for Ontario's wine industry. By the advent of the 20th century, the Niagara Peninsula boasted close to 2,025 hectares under vine. But two events set the burgeoning wine industry off on a path of incipient self-destruction: the First World War and Prohibition. When the war broke out, the government's need for industrial alcohol to make explosives synchronized with the popular sentiment for Prohibition, and within two years, the distilleries were converted to the production of industrial alcohol for the war effort. The Ontario Temperance Act was passed on September 15, 1916, by the government of Sir William F. Hearst, himself an active Methodist layman

An autumn mist settles on the vineyards of Hidden Bench Winery on Niagara's Beamsville Bench.

and dedicated temperance advocate. All bars, clubs and liquor stores would be closed for the duration of the war. Amazingly, a strong grape growers' lobby managed to have native wines exempted from the provisions, and wine became the only alcoholic beverage that could be sold legally in the province.

Wᴴᴇɴ ᴘʀᴏʜɪʙɪᴛɪᴏɴ ᴡᴀꜱ introduced, there were 10 operating wineries in Ontario. When it ended on October 31, 1927, the Board of Liquor Commissioners had granted no fewer than 47 licences. Prohibition, more than any other factor, had turned Canadians into a nation of wine drinkers. In 1920, some 21 million Canadians consumed 221,985

gallons of domestic wine. A decade later, the figure was 2,208,807 gallons — for Ontario alone. The favourite by far (preferred by 80 percent of Canadians) was a red port-style wine of maximum alcoholic strength made from Concord grapes. (These products were known affectionately as "Block & Tackle wines" — after consuming a bottle, you could walk a block and tackle anyone.)

In an effort to regulate both the production of wine and the growing public consumption, the government created the Liquor Control Board of Ontario, with the emphasis on control. Big companies such as Brights and Jordan

began buying up the licences of less viable operations — not for their equipment or stock but for the retail store that each winery was allowed to operate. Through these amalgamations, the number of wineries in Ontario was reduced from 61 to 8; and no new licences would be granted until 1975, when two small boutique operations were started — Inniskillin and a sparkling-wine facility named Podamer.

These two fledgling wineries joined the Big Six: Andrés, Barnes, Brights, Château-Gai, Jordan and London.

Ontario wines were still being made from labrusca varieties and hybrids, such as Maréchal Foch, Baco Noir, Seyval Blanc and Vidal. Although Brights had been experimenting with Chardonnay as early as 1955, the Horticultural Research Institute in

The gentle hills of Beamsville border the Niagara Escarpment and are a delight for photographers and weekend visitors.

Content Act of 1972. Two years before, Andrés had sold off the Ontario vineyards it had purchased in 1962, and Brights soon followed Andrés' lead.

A few dedicated growers, including Bill Lenko and John Marynissen, defied the conventional wisdom and planted Chardonnay and Cabernet Sauvignon in their Niagara Peninsula vineyards, while a youthful nurseryman named Donald Ziraldo supplied interested growers with vinifera plants from his Niagara-on-the-Lake farm. Hermann Weis, who owns St. Urbans-Hof winery in the Mosel, a German wine region, provided his Weis clone Riesling to interested growers and eventually set up his own winery, Vineland Estates, in Ontario.

The seminal event in Ontario's wine story occurred in 1974, when Donald Ziraldo and his Austrian partner, Karl Kaiser, made the first batch of Maréchal Foch from their own grapes in a converted barn on the Niagara Parkway. The following year, they got their licence as Inniskillin and moved to their current location just west of the Ziraldo nursery. The co-founders of Ontario's first new winery since Prohibition had one clear standard: They would use 100 percent locally grown wines, preferably vinifera. Inniskillin became the model for an exciting new breed of estate or farm wineries that made wines from their own vineyards: Château des Charmes (1978), Newark (1979, now Trius), Reif Estate (1982), Vineland Estates (1983), Konzelmann Estates (1984), Stoney Ridge (1985), Cave Spring Cellars (1986) and Henry of Pelham (1988).

The philosophies and practices of these new vintners were enshrined in the regulations of the Vintners Quality Alliance (VQA), the single most important piece of legislation to save the industry from extinction. The small players

Vineland warned growers against planting vinifera varietals, which, it said, could not survive Canadian winters. The major thrust of the commercial wineries was to blend offshore wines with their locally grown product, a practice legitimized by the Ontario Wine

Fine dining is on offer at the Peller Estates Winery Restaurant, above. An aerial view of the Niagara Peninsula's Château des Charmes estate, opposite, provides an impressive perspective on a Canadian institution.

Once Ontario's VQA wines began to win medals in international competitions — and, more important, the hearts and taste buds of Ontario consumers — new entrepreneurs emerged to start their own wineries. Between 1990 and 2003, the total rose to 36. This second wave of small wineries included farmers who saw bigger profits from making wine than from selling their grapes to the major wineries. It also included second careerists who had been successful in other enterprises and looked at wineries as both an investment and a lifestyle choice.

While the old guard were influenced by their winemaking experience in France and Germany or by their taste for European wines, the new winemakers were more New World in their vision. They had been trained in oenology in Australia (Joe Will at Strewn, Sue-Ann Staff at Staff Estate), had winemaking experience in South Africa, New Zealand and the United States or were the first graduates of the Cool Climate Oenology and Viticulture Institute (CCOVI) and Niagara College.

Currently, the industry is redefining itself with sub-appellations in the Niagara Peninsula, an exercise in differentiating soil types and microclimates, which will add another layer of sophistication and complexity to consumer choice. The emergence of a third viticultural area in Ontario, Prince Edward County, to join Niagara Peninsula and Lake Erie North Shore is only the beginning of this quest for new and less costly land on which to plant vineyards. Already intrepid growers are moving as far north as Thunder Bay, Owen Sound, Roseneath and Collingwood and as far east as Chesterville. With global warming, who knows how far north vineyards will be planted in the future?

had become the engine that propelled Ontario wines, dragging the large commercial players reluctantly along in their combined wake.

The small estate wineries captured consumers' palates, and the Big Six found their market share eaten into by these new upstarts. To increase revenues, the Big Six expanded into other provinces and began to consolidate. Brights bought Jordan; Château-Gai snapped up Barnes. In 1989, a buyout of Château-Gai from Labatt by a team of its managers, led by Allan Jackson and Don Triggs, created Cartier Wines, a company destined to swallow up Inniskillin, Brights and London before turning its gaze on British Columbia, Quebec and then the world.

Angels Gate Winery

In 1995, a group of 13 Bay Street investors with a passion for wine planted a 5-hectare vineyard on land once owned by the Congregation of Missionary Sisters of Christian Charity — hence the angelic connection. In the 1950s, the property had seen service as a mink farm but was abandoned when fur fell out of favour. A new mission-style winery was built in 2001 and opened for visitors a year later. Aussie winemaker Philip Dowell now presides over 73 hectares, from which he produces Pinot Noir, Riesling, Cabernet Franc, old vine Chardonnay and sparkling wines under the Archangel label.

Angels Gate Winery
4260 Mountainview Road
Beamsville, ON L0R 1B2
(905) 486-1075
angelsgatewinery.com

Cave Spring Cellars

Cave Spring Cellars
3836 Main Street
Jordan, ON L0R 1S0
(888) 806-9910
(905) 562-3581
cavespring.ca

IMAGINE HAVING A winery on the main street of your village—and one of wine country's best restaurants to boot. Cave Spring, in Jordan Village, a much-visited tourist destination in the Niagara region, is housed in a gracious greystone building, originally an apple warehouse that dates back to 1870. The entire enterprise—winery, restaurant and luxury inn on the other side of the street—has its foundation on 70 hectares of benchland vineyards planted in 1978 by John Pennachetti and his son Len. Father and son discovered the original site by scouting the area in a small plane. In 1981, recognizing the potential of Niagara's nascent wine industry, Len, who today is the president of the company, built a house in the vineyard.

The Wine Council of Ontario's Linda Watts, opposite, pays a visit to the "press room" in Cave Spring's historic 19th-century facility.

Niagara Peninsula

Len Pennachetti, president of Cave Spring Cellars.

"I saw a chance for getting back to the land and creating a place where our family could do something special," says Len, whose family now owns 78 hectares of vineyards on the bench of the escarpment. "There's an allure in cultivating vineyards — you're literally putting down roots. They exist from generation to generation. The way they grow and evolve reflects all the energy and commitment you put into them. What better family business could there be?"

In 1986, with mature vinifera vines at their disposal, father and son teamed up with winemaker Angelo Pavan, a friend of Len's since childhood, and Tom Muckle (also a founding partner of Thirty Bench Vineyards) to open a winery that bears the name of the

farm located on the slope above the village. Their first estate-grown Riesling and Chardonnay heralded the quality that has been consistent ever since. The partners' Italian heritage has found expression in the production of an *appassimento* red wine they call

La Penna (*appassimento* is an ancient Italian traditional practice of increasing the sugars in freshly picked grapes by allowing them to dry for a matter of weeks before fermentation).

A much-awarded winemaker, Angelo produces some of the best Chardonnay, sparkling wine and dry and sweet Riesling in the country. In 2011, he celebrated 25 years of commanding the cellars at Cave Spring. No other winemaker in Canada has served as winemaker at the same winery for so long.

Château des Charmes

Château des Charmes
1025 York Road
Niagara-on-the-Lake, ON L0S 1P0
(905) 262-4219
chateaudescharmes.com

AUL MICHEL BOSC, a fifth-generation winemaker from Algeria by way of France, is a major figure in the pioneering efforts of the modern Canadian wine industry — efforts for which he received the Order of Canada in 2005. Given its founder's history, it's not surprising that Château des Charmes' home is a copper-roofed château that would not be out of place in the Loire Valley. There is an undeniable sense of grandeur as you enter the main door to see the curved staircase and the well-appointed tasting room on the ground floor.

After studying oenology at the University of Dijon in Burgundy and subsequently managing a large wine cooperative in Algeria, Paul immigrated to Canada in 1963. He began his illustrious winemaking career in Canada with Château-Gai Wines (which eventually became Vincor) before creating his own winery with his lawyer-partner Rodger Gordon in 1978. The original winery was an unprepossessing cement-block

Paul Michel Bosc and his son Paul-André Bosc, opposite.

bunker set in the vineyard, but with the success of Paul's wines came the financing to buy vineyard land in St. David's and, in 1994, to build the landmark château in which to house a new winery facility.

With his wife Andrée, son Paul-André and daughter-in-law Michèle, Paul has created an impressive portfolio of Château des Charmes wines in the French style. From the winery's four separate vineyards, which total 105 hectares, he has introduced several new varieties, including Aligoté, Viognier and Savagnin, to the province. From his original vineyard, Paul has developed Gamay Droit, a new clone of Gamay. He has long affiliated himself and his company with organizations such as the National Research Council to support research projects that range from carbonic maceration, clonal selection and reverse osmosis to new canopy management techniques and climate control through the use of wind-machine technology.

A dedicated equestrian with his own horse-breeding stable, Paul has named his flagship Bordeaux blend Equuleus, after the constellation whose Latin name translates as "little horse." In the family's experimental vineyard, more than 1,000 new vitis vinifera species have been created over a decade by crossing such established varieties as Pinot Noir with Gamay Noir. One cross of two red varieties had unexpected results, producing red grapes one vintage, then alternating between red and white on subsequent vintages. The number of these experimental vines have been whittled down over the years to about 200 as the Boscs try to propagate viable new wine grapes. With its traditional varietals, Château des Charmes regularly wins gold medals at the Ontario Wine Awards for its Late Harvest Rieslings and Icewines.

Creekside Estate Winery

Originally called VP Cellars, Creekside was purchased by Laura McCain in 1998. A succession of Australian winemakers established a reputation for producing big bold red wines and flavourful Sauvignon Blanc from Creekside's 24.6 hectares of vines. They were the first to plant Shiraz (Syrah) in Ontario, and today their Broken Press Shiraz waltzes away with gold medals. Rob Power, who has been making wine here since 2002, is one of the most accomplished vintners in Canada. In 2012, Laura sold Creekside to the Equity Wine Group, but her name remains as two delicious blends, Laura's White and Laura's Red.

Creekside Estate Winery
2170 Fourth Avenue
Jordan Station, ON L0R 1S0
(877) 262-9463
(905) 562-0035
creeksidewine.com

Fielding Estate Winery

Ken and Marg Fielding established their winery in 2002, housing it in a structure that blends contemporary Canadiana design with the warmth and feel of cottage country. From the tasting bar, large glass panels afford a unique view of the winery operations and a breathtaking view across Lake Ontario. Winemaker Richie Roberts's wide and varied portfolio sources fruit from 20 hectares of vines. Richie's Rieslings and Pinot Gris are exemplary. And don't miss Fielding's Rock Pile Pinot Gris. Its flagship wines are bottled under the Chosen FEW label and are made from the best barrels of top vintages.

Fielding Estate Winery
4020 Locust Lane
Beamsville, ON L0R 1B2
(888) 778-7758
(905) 563-0668
fieldingwines.com

Flat Rock Cellars

Flat Rock Cellars
2727 Seventh Avenue
Jordan, ON L0R 1S0
(905) 562-8994
flatrockcellars.com

LOOK CLOSELY AT the logo on the label of a Flat Rock wine, and you'll see the stylized image of a woman holding a basket of grapes. "To us," says company president Ed Madronich Jr., "she is the embodiment of winemaking. Our predominant colour is red because it is not only the colour of wine but also of passion, and we are nothing if not passionate about winemaking!"

Set into the side of a hill high on the escarpment, this striking contemporary winery comprises two six-sided spaces linked by a bridge over a five-storey, gravity-flow facility in concrete, steel, wood and glass. It enjoys a commanding view of the 32-hectare vineyard. The wine shop, erected on enormous steel legs, is on two levels and offers a 360-degree panoramic view through its windows. Named for the huge flat rocks that were excavated from the site to make room for drainage tiles under

Ed Madronich in his ultra-modern gravity-flow winery.

each row of vines, the winery has a geo-thermal heating and cooling system involving 4,575 metres of piping — just one of the innovative technologies in this space-age facility.

Australian Darryl Brooker made an immediate impression with his maiden vintage here in 2003, especially with his Riesling and Pinot Noir. When he was hired away by Hillebrand, another Australian winemaker, Vicky Louise Bartier, from the Barossa Valley, came on board for the 2005 vintage. She was followed by Marlize Beyers, a South African, and New Zealander Ross Wise — which goes to show just how international the Ontario wine industry has become. Since 2012, Jay Johnson,

a graduate of Niagara College's Winery and Viticulture program, has been making the wines at Flat Rock Cellars. Flat Rock was the first winery in Ontario to bottle its entire portfolio of wines under screw-cap closures, including its Icewine (a world first). Nadja's Vineyard, named for the founder's wife, produces one of the best Rieslings in Canada. Ed Madronich Jr., who runs the winery with his father, describes the experience for the visitor as "fun, welcoming, approachable and unpretentious." Whether you're a fan of contemporary architecture or you just love wine, don't miss Flat Rock.

Henry of Pelham Family Estate Winery

**Henry of Pelham
Family Estate Winery**
1469 Pelham Road Street, RR 1
St. Catharines, ON L2R 6P7
(877) 735-4267
(905) 684 8423
henryofpelham.com

THE YOUTHFUL EXUBERANCE of the Speck brothers, Paul, Matthew and Daniel, finds expression in their easy-drinking Sibling Rivalry label — three blends with three grapes in a white, a red and a rosé. The brothers have run this winery with its close to 70 hectares of vineyards since the premature death of their father in 1993. Paul Speck Sr. was an educator who, in 1982, bought the property that had belonged to his ancestors as far back as 1794. The original owner was Nicholas Smith, whose son Henry (after whom the winery is named) built a coaching inn in 1842. That historic building is now the winery's tasting room, wine store and restaurant. Back in the early 1980s, the Specks were in the winemaking vanguard — they were planting vinifera grapes when other growers were relying on native North American

Winemaker Ron Giesbrecht, opposite, harvests Icewine grapes.

varieties like Concord and Niagara. They proved themselves to be venturesome on another front as well: Henry of Pelham was the first Ontario winery to introduce screw caps for its premium Barrel-Fermented Chardonnay in 2003.

Its long-serving winemaker, Ron Giesbrecht, has gone from strength to strength, producing some of the best wines in the province and making an intense, flavourful Baco Noir — the Reserve is a signature wine for Henry of Pelham. Ron's top wines are the Speck Family Reserve Chardonnay, Pinot Noir and Cabernet/Merlot blend. These wines are a selection of the best barrels produced from low-yielding vines over 20 years old. There is also a Riesling under this label that is not aged in oak. Of particular note are Henry of Pelham's sparkling wines under the Cuvée Catharine label, a non-vintage Brut and a Rosé Brut; in 2013, a vintage-dated Blanc de Blancs will be added to the portfolio. Don't miss the Canadian art gallery in the coaching inn, where tastings with Canadian cheeses, as well as tours and sales, are now conducted.

Hidden Bench Vineyards and Winery

**Hidden Bench
Vineyards and Winery**
4152 Locust Lane
Beamsville, ON L0R 1B0
(905) 563-8700
hiddenbench.com

Mᴏɴᴛʀᴇ́ᴀʟ-ʙᴏʀɴ ʟᴀᴡʏᴇʀ Harald Thiel sold his flourishing audio-visual services company in 2003 to become a vintner. "I have always had an interest in wine from a very young age," says Harald. "My interest gelled in 1980–81 when I studied for a year in France and had the opportunity to sample some memorable wines and to tour the winemaking regions." As a successful businessman, Harald's passion for wine led him to found the Gourmet Food and Wine Show in Toronto, but eventually, he wanted to get even closer to the wine business. He spent 18 months looking for suitable properties in Niagara before purchasing the 11.5-hectare Locust Lane Vineyard in 2003 (the home vineyard was planted in 1998). In 2004, he bought the then mature 10.5-hectare Rosomel Vineyard, which had been planted in 1976. Finally, in 2007, he took possession of

Harald Thiel with his German shorthaired pointer, Bismarck, opposite.

the 14.5-hectare Felseck Vineyard, which had been planted from 1988 through 2008. All three vineyards are located on the Beamsville Bench and are farmed organically, having been certified organic since 2010. As an estate winery, Hidden Bench only produces wines with grapes that have been grown in its three estate vineyards. The current production of 8,000 cases per year should eventually reach 10,000 cases in 2014.

When the winery opened in 2005, Harald engaged Jean-Martin Bouchard as winemaker, a fellow Québecois who created an instant reputation for Hidden Bench's red blends, Terroir Caché and La Brunante, as well as the white Meritage blend, Nuit Blanche. When J-M, as he is known, left for British Columbia in 2009 to become Road 13's winemaker, Harald hired Marlize Beyers from Flat Rock Cellars. Marlize has carried on the tradition of making superlative wines across the entire portfolio. The Pinot Noirs, Chardonnays and Rieslings are particularly impressive and constitute 85 percent of the total estate production. Attention to detail from vineyard to bottle shows that this operation aims at and produces only the highest quality wine.

Inniskillin Wines

Inniskillin Wines
Niagara-on-the-Lake
ON L0S 1J0
(888) 466-4754
(905) 468-2187
inniskillin.com

THE FOUNDING FATHERS Donald Ziraldo and Karl Kaiser may have left the building in 2006, but they continue to cast a long, beneficent shadow, not only over Inniskillin but over the entire Ontario wine industry. The international recognition that Canadian Icewine has received is due to their joint efforts.

On July 31, 1975, Karl Kaiser and Donald Ziraldo were granted the first winery licence in Ontario since 1929. The story of how it happened is worth retelling here. The flamboyant extreme skier Donald Ziraldo received his degree in agriculture from the

University of Guelph in 1971 and began running the family nursery, which specialized in fruit trees and grapevines. The stolid academic Karl Kaiser, a native of Austria, once studied for the priesthood, but the church's loss was the Ontario wine lover's gain. Abandoning ecclesiastical pursuits, Karl moved to Canada in 1968 after meeting and marrying his Canadian wife Silvia. A dedicated home winemaker with a degree in chemistry, Karl met Donald

when he visited the nursery to buy some French hybrid vines. The two men, so different in temperament, struck up a friendship and talked for hours about Ontario wine over a bottle of Karl's homemade product. After a lot of dreaming and talking, they decided to apply for a winery licence.

"The late General George Kitching, chairman of the Liquor Control Board of Ontario, shared our vision of creating a premium estate winery

producing varietal wines from grapes grown in the Niagara Peninsula," recalls Donald. Their first red wine was a Maréchal Foch 1974 that they called Vin Nouveau. Ten years later, this initial effort was still very much alive and tasted like an old Burgundy.

The original Inniskillin winery was housed in a packing shed at the Ziraldo family nursery, a couple of kilometres east of its current location. The property's first owner had been a Colonel Cooper, who served in an Irish regiment, the Inniskilling Fusiliers, during the War of 1812. On completing his military service, he was granted Crown land, which he named the Inniskillin Farm.

In 1978, Donald and Karl relocated to the winery's present site, the Brae Burn Estate. The contemporary Inniskillin winery combines the partners' experience, featuring architectural features of both Old World and New World wine regions that merge seamlessly with the surrounding vineyards. The historic barn, thought to have been designed by Frank Lloyd Wright, contains the shop and tasting room on the ground floor, while a huge loft above is used to host private receptions. A smaller adjacent barn, part of the self-guided tour, is now a museum.

To Inniskillin goes the credit of creating the international market for Canadian Icewine,

with the awarding of a major prize to its Vidal 1989 at the 1991 Vinexpo in Bordeaux. In addition, Karl was the first Ontario winemaker to make a vineyard-designated Chardonnay in the Burgundian style (at one time, Inniskillin had five single-vineyard Chardonnays) and to champion Pinot Noir as a great grape for Ontario's climate.

In 1993, Inniskillin was the first Canadian winery to enter into a joint-production venture with a French company when it invited Jaffelin's Burgundy specialist, Bernard Repolt, to help select the best barrels of its Chardonnay and Pinot Noir for a label called Alliance.

Karl now concentrates on Inniskillin's Icewine production in both Ontario and British Columbia, leaving the day-to-day winemaking decisions for the rest of the portfolio to others, first to Australian Philip Dowell, and then to his Aussie colleague James Manners. When Karl Kaiser retired in 2006, Bruce Nicholson took over the role as winemaker after a highly successful (and medal-laden) 13-year career as head winemaker at Jackson-Triggs' Okanagan operation.

Purchased by Cartier in 1992, Inniskillin formed the nucleus of the company that soon became Vincor International, which was in turn purchased by Constellation in 2006.

Donald Ziraldo and Karl Kaiser

Impresarios of Icewine

Karl Kaiser (at left) and Donald Ziraldo.

THE MARCH 1998 issue of *Wine Tidings* magazine featured a smiling Donald Ziraldo on its cover. Wearing a black baseball cap with the Inniskillin logo picked out in gold letters, Donald was seated on the Great Wall of China with a bottle of Inniskillin Vidal Icewine and a glass by his side. The headline read: "Inniskillin Icewine Cracks China."

That was typical Donald Ziraldo — showman, salesman, promoter, merchant-traveller, ambassador — bringing the message of Canadian wines to the world at a time when his peers were at home worrying whether they could compete with California. On that trip, Donald visited Beijing, Shanghai, Singapore and Hong Kong, opening up Asian markets to Inniskillin Icewine and paving the way for his competitors.

Ask any foreigner to name a Canadian winery, and in an instant, they will answer "Inniskillin." No one has done a better job beating the drum for Canadian wines while furthering the interests of the winery than Donald and his long-time partner Karl Kaiser. Founded in 1974, Inniskillin was the first winery start-up in Ontario since Prohibition and the trailblazer for all those small farm wineries that followed.

While his winemaker-partner Karl laboured in the cellar and the laboratory, Donald travelled the world, carrying with him wines for all to taste. An avid skier, he did a lot of his business on the slopes of Europe, New Zealand and Vale, Colorado. "It's a natural relationship, and after all, 'ski' is in the middle of Inniskillin," quips Donald, who collects Art Deco objets d'art and is a vocal defender of Niagara region's agricultural land. The founding chairman of the VQA, he was instrumental in creating Brock University's Cool Climate Oenology and Viticulture Institute, which is housed in Inniskillin Hall. For his contributions to the Canadian wine industry, Donald was awarded the Order of Canada in 1993.

When Vincor (which owned Inniskillin as well as Jackson-Triggs) was sold to Constellation in 2006, both Donald and Karl subsequently retired from Inniskillin. Donald is currently the managing director of Senhora do Convento, a port lodge in Portugal's Douro Valley, and runs his own boutique winery in Niagara, Equifera Estate. Karl consults to Inniskillin's winemaker, Bruce Nicholson, on Icewine production and is a much sought-after lecturer on the subject.

Jackson-Triggs Niagara Estate Winery and Le Clos Jordanne

**Jackson-Triggs
Niagara Estate Winery**
2145 Niagara Stone Road
(Regional Road 55), RR 3
Niagara-on-the-Lake, ON L0S 1J0
(866) 589-4637
(905) 468-4637
jacksontriggswinery.com

Le Clos Jordanne
(905) 562-9404
leclosjordanne.com

NAMED FOR VINCOR founding partners Don Triggs and Allan Jackson, the Jackson-Triggs label first appeared in 1993, but it wasn't until 2001 that the large port- folio of wines got its own dedicated winery. That year, Jackson-Triggs opened its spectacular ultra-contemporary winery on the highway into Niagara-on-the-Lake. The three- tiered, gravity-flow facility covers 4,370 square metres and is set back from the road in its own 5-hectare vineyard. The design was inspired by traditional farm buildings, with their post-and-beam frames and wide barn doors, although some visitors think the structure looks more like an airport terminal building. Its materials are a combination of natural stone at its base, high-tech aluminum framing, native fir roof trusses and vast windows that showcase the vineyard at every turn. The

Trained in France, winemaker Sébastien Jacquey, above, and at work in the vineyard, page 138, heads the production of acclaimed Chardonnays and Pinot Noirs at Le Clos Jordanne. Winemaker Marco Piccoli, opposite, verifies recent cuvées in the Jackson-Triggs cellar.

vaulted underground cellar, with its tiers of French and American oak barrels, is impressive, and visitors can enjoy food and wine pairings in the tasting gallery. The 1,000 square metres of Pinot Noir vines planted at the entrance to the winery in 2001 are dedicated to Adrienne Clarkson, the former Governor General of Canada. Proceeds from the sale of this small block are donated in perpetuity to a charity of the present incumbent's choice.

Jackson-Triggs produces a large portfolio of wines under four price categories: Proprietors' Selection (600,000 cases) and three VQA tiers (120,400 cases) — Reserve Series, Grand Reserve and the flagship Delaine, which was a vineyard planted, owned and named for Don and Elaine Triggs in 1999. The 38 hectares are planted to Pinot Noir, Cabernet Sauvignon, Merlot, Cabernet Franc and Syrah. The white varietals are Chardonnay, Riesling, Sauvignon Blanc, Gewürztraminer and Sémillon. The winery buys fruit from 20 to 24 growers annually.

In 2000, Jackson-Triggs entered into a joint venture with the giant Burgundy shipper Boisset to produce Burgundy-style Chardonnay and Pinot Noir from a 14-hectare vineyard to be called Le Clos Jordan. After an appeal from the Jordan winery in Sonoma, California, however, they were obliged to

change the name to Jordanne. Over the years, the winery has acquired other vineyard lots and now numbers 41 hectares with long-term leases on a further 11 hectares. Le Clos Jordanne's single vineyard wines, originally produced by winemaker Thomas Bach-elder and now by Sébastien Jacquey, display distinctive terroir differences and are con-sistently some of the best Chardonnays and Pinot Noirs to be had in Canada. Currently, Le Clos Jordanne operates out of an indus-trial building on the QEW (Queen Elizabeth Highway) that is not open to the public.

Malivoire Wine Company

Malivoire Wine Company
4260 King Street East
Beamsville, ON L0R 1B0
(866) 644-2244
(905) 563-9253
malivoire.com

Whas Martin Malivoire and Moira Saganski went looking for vineyard land in the Niagara Peninsula in 1993, it took them two years to find the perfect sites. The first acquisition would become the Moira Vineyard (acclaimed for its Chardonnay and Gewürztraminer); the other was to be the home vineyard of the winery facility. Together they total 20 hectares. Martin and Moira also source grapes from the Epp and Eastman vineyards, which adds another 7 hectares. As an engineer and former special effects wizard for movies, Martin designed an unusual state-of-the-art facility — three attached Quonset huts set on a hillside with a 10-metre drop to allow a gravity-flow operation (the wine is gentled along at each stage from crush to tank to barrel without the use of pumps). The entranceway, with its local stone pillars and rock gardens, softens the utilitarian lines of the compactly designed facility. A barrel cellar that maintains the architectural integrity of the site was added

Winemaker Shiraz Mottiar, a strong believer in minimal manipulations, punches down the cap during Pinot Noir fermentation, opposite.

later: It, too, is an elongated Quonset hut, set half underground and insulated to maintain a constant cool temperature of 12°C. Maliviore's distinctive labels feature the company's controversial logo — a ladybug (which is also the name of their rosé). The insect is used in the Moira Vineyard instead of insecticides but is unrelated to the Asian ladybug, which compromised a portion of Niagara's 2001 vintage.

From the outset, Martin wanted to produce the best rosé in Canada, and with the help of his first winemaker Ann Sperling (now at Southbrook), he achieved that goal. In August 2005, Shiraz Mottiar took over as winemaker.

Shiraz was one of the first graduates from Brock University's Cool Climate Oenology and Viticulture Institute in 2000. In 2002, he flew to Australia's Yarra Valley to participate in the crush at Coldstream Hills. James Halliday, the winery's founder and wine judge, described Shiraz Mottiar in his book *Wine Odyssey: A year of wine, food and travel* as "one of the stars of the vintage." Shiraz has lived up to that early praise, producing top-flight Chardonnay, Gamay and Gewürztraminer. He also makes what must be the world's most expensive Passe-Tout-Grains — a blend of Pinot Noir and Gamay called The Cat on the Bench Pinot Noir, which sells for $100 a bottle.

Niagara College Teaching Winery

Niagara College offers a three-year course that gives students a working knowledge of all aspects of grape growing, vineyard management and wine-making. Winemaker Terence van Rooyen teaches the next generation how to coax the best flavours out of Ontario grapes, and he's confident enough in the results that the class sells their wine in the campus store. Not only have these wines done very well in competitions such as the Canadian and the Ontario Wine Awards, but they are priced to sell. As a result, the 5,000 cases move quickly. Proceeds from the sale help to finance the college's horticulture and agribusiness programs.

Niagara College Teaching Winery
135 Taylor Road
Niagara-on-the-Lake, ON L0S 1J0
(905) 641-2252, ext. 4070
niagaracollegewine.ca

143

Peller Estates and Trius Winery at Hillebrand

Peller Estates
290 John Street East
Niagara-on-the-Lake, ON L0S 1J0
(905) 468-4678

Trius Winery at Hillebrand
1249 Niagara Stone Road
(Regional Road 55)
Niagara-on-the-Lake, ON L0S 1J0
(800) 582-8412
(905) 468-7123

hillebrand.com

PELLER ESTATES USED to be called Andrés Wines, a name synonymous with Baby Duck, probably the first wine that most Canadians growing up in the 1970s and 1980s ever tasted. The company was founded by Andrew Peller, a Hungarian immigrant. He opened the British Columbia plant in Port Moody in 1961 and the Ontario plant in 1969. To distance itself from the Baby Duck image, the company created the Peller Estates label in 1997 and built a monumental château-style winery, also called Peller Estates, in Niagara-on-the-Lake. The Peller family also owns Trius Winery at Hillebrand and Thirty Bench in Ontario, and Calona, Sandhill and Red Rooster in British Columbia.

Trius Winery at Hillebrand has undergone a number of reincarnations since 1979, when Joe Pohorly created a small farm winery called Newark on the highway leading into Niagara-on-the-Lake. Joe sold Newark to the Swiss bitters company, Underberg, which renamed the property Hillebrand Estates and capitalized it lavishly by the standards of the day. In 1994, Underberg sold the company to Andrés, which continued the expansion. Today, the winery complex looks like a colonial settlement of sand-coloured buildings,

with the vineyards stretching out far behind. In fact, the company owns just under a hectare of Chardonnay and Riesling here. It has 67 hectares in total and contracts 65 growers to supply it with grapes.

During his 15 years as winemaker, J.L. Groulx did much to give the wines a stylish French profile, especially with the Trius label, before being wooed away to the new Stratus winery in 2004. Following him was the talented Australian Darryl Brooker, who had been the first winemaker at Flat Rock Cellars. When Darryl

Niagara Peninsula

left to join CedarCreek in the Okanagan, the company hired the award-winning winemaker Craig MacDonald away from Creekside. Such is the Canadian wine industry's equivalent of musical chairs. The Trius brand has become so recognizable that in the spring of 2012, the company put that name front and centre on their signage. With its fine dining restaurant and popular series of outdoor jazz, blues and classical concerts, Hillebrand has led the way in promoting agri-tourism in the Niagara area. These events are extremely popular in the summer months. Visitors bring their lawn furniture and umbrellas and picnic on the grass while listening to great Canadian performers. Hillebrand also offers one of the best winery tours in the Niagara Peninsula.

Peninsula Ridge Estates Winery

**Peninsula Ridge
Estates Winery**
5600 King Street West
PO Box 500
Beamsville, ON L0R 1B0
(905) 563-0900
peninsularidge.com

WHEN HE LEFT a highly successful career in the petroleum industry, Norman Beal had no intention of opening a winery in Ontario. His idea was to buy properties in California and New York State. But at the urging of family members, he abandoned the notion of investing in the United States, left Connecticut, where he'd been living, and came home to Ontario to create Peninsula Ridge at a cost of $4.5 million. He bought the Beamsville property in March 1999, with its beautifully sited Victorian farmhouse (it looks not unlike a non-threatening version of the Bates family home in *Psycho*). Initially, Norm planted 16 hectares of vineyard on the home property (a former apple orchard) and purchased an additional 8 hectares next door to the winery, planting this to Merlot and Chardonnay in 2001. One of the winery's remarkable features is the magnificent

Owner Norman Beal assesses a red wine in Peninsula Ridge's fresco-decorated underground cellar.

353-square-metre, L-shaped underground cellar. Today, the sophisticated Restaurant at Peninsula Ridge is housed in a farmhouse known as the William D. Kitchen House, while the retail store and tasting bar are located in a tastefully restored 1855 post-and-beam barn. The coach house that stands behind the farmhouse is used for private and corporate events and for weddings catered by the restaurant's chefs.

In 2007, Peninsula Ridge Estates teamed up with Nancy and Patrick McNally, who are among the top grape growers on the Beamsville Bench. "Nancy McNally's early entry into farming provided her with the skills, background and passion needed to produce the highest quality grapes," says Norm. "The McNallys currently have over 20 hectares of vinifera vines under cultivation that are exclusive to Peninsula Ridge." From the winery's opening in 2000 through 2009, Jean-Pierre Colas presided over the cellar. Currently, Jamie Evans, a graduate of Brock University's Cool Climate Oenology and Viticultural Institute, makes the wine here — a far cry from his original ambition to become an archaeologist. For several years, Jamie was Joe Will's assistant winemaker at Strewn.

Pillitteri Estates Winery

Pillitteri's Jeff Letvenuk harvests Cabernet Franc grapes for Icewine.

Pillitteri Estates Winery
1696 Niagara Stone Road
(Regional Road 55), RR 2
Niagara-on-the-Lake, ON L0S 1J0
(905) 468-3147
pillitteri.com

THE CARRETTO, AN antique Sicilian donkey cart that has pride of place in the winery's Awards Room, speaks to founder Gary Orazio Vincenzo Pillitteri's heritage. Gary (the federal MP for Niagara Falls from 1993 through 2004) and his three brothers were all born in Sicily. The Pillitteris emigrated from Italy in the mid-20th century, and their mother, a proud Sicilian, gave each of her sons a carretto as a remembrance of their family history. The largest and most beautifully decorated of these was donated by the family to the Museum of Civilization in Ottawa in 1989, where it can be seen today.

A grape grower since his arrival in the Niagara region, Gary Pillitteri was also an enthusiastic amateur winemaker whose success with Icewine in a local competition encouraged him to start his own commercial operation in 1993. Now Pillitteri is an all-family enterprise, with siblings, cousins and friends contributing grapes and expertise on the 80-hectare property. The winery complex, with its farmer's market, wraparound balcony, trophy area and five tasting bars, has been designed to accommodate large numbers of visitors and to avoid the problem of overcrowding at what has become an extremely popular venue. Its architectural look, according to Gary's son Charlie, is "Old World conversing with New World"—the idea of traditional winery design with contemporary styling. A feature worthy of the *Guinness Book of Records* is the 12.7-metre concrete tasting table in the Roman-vaulted barrel cellar, set with 23 chairs (23 happens to be Gary's lucky number). The wine library features past vintages of Pillitteri wines, examples of Ontario wines from other estates and Charlie Pillitteri's personal collection.

The flagship wine at Pillitteri is Icewine—there are 13 different varieties, including the sumptuously packaged Exclamation Series. The category accounts for 60 percent of Pillitteri's production, and it's sold to 19 countries around the world. In fact, Pillitteri may be the world's largest family estate producer and exporter of Icewine. The high level of production was originally set by Sue-Ann Staff, who left the winery to manage the short-lived 20 Bees co-operative in 2004 and then opened her eponymous winery in 2009. Aleksandar Kolundzic (formerly with Jackson-Triggs) now heads up the Pillitteri winemaking team.

PondView Estate Winery

The Puglisi family, originally from Sicily, has been farming 24.2 hectares of vines in what is now the Four Mile Creek sub-appellation since 1974. Lou, the son of immigrant Giuseppe Puglisi, was elected Grape King in 2008 for maintaining "the best vineyard in Ontario"; a year later, he opened the family winery with Fred Di Profio as winemaker (Fred went on to open his own winery in 2012). The Bella Terra series of Pond-View wines — Chardonnay, Pinot Gris and Cabernet Sauvignon — continue to garner medals, as does the Vidal Icewine.

PondView Estate Winery
925 Line 2
Niagara-on-the-Lake, ON L0S 1J0
(905) 468-0777
pondviewwinery.com

Lou Puglisi harvests his Vidal grapes for Icewine.

Ravine Vineyard

Ravine Vineyard
1366 York Road
St. David's, ON L0S 1P0
(905) 562-8853
ravinevineyard.com

IF EVER A new winery hit the road running, as it were, it could be said to be Ravine Vineyard. The winery, founded in 2006, may be young, but as a vineyard site, it has one of the longest histories in the province. David Jackson Lowrey established a farm here in 1867, and two years later, he planted 50 vines. Today, that sense of the past is evoked by the William Woodruff House, which dates back to the turn of the 19th century. The 325-square-metre building was moved piecemeal from Port Hope, Ontario, and lovingly restored and reassembled on the farm in 2007. This magnificent old wood-framed house is now the winery's hospitality centre, tasting room and retail store. Adjacent to it is the Ravine Vineyard restaurant, a French bistro and deli, presided over by Chef Paul Harber, the owners' son.

For generations, the family sold their grapes — labrusca and French hybrids — to Brights Wines. In 2003, after allowing the vineyard to lay fallow for several years, Norma Jane, a Lowrey, and her husband Blair Harber replanted their property to Cabernet Franc, Cabernet Sauvignon, Merlot, Chardonnay, Sauvignon Blanc, Riesling and Gewürztraminer on the advice of their consulting oenologist, Peter Gamble. The 14 hectares of vines are farmed both organically and biodynamically, and the day-to-day winemaking operations are conducted by Shauna White, the niece of Ann Sperling. The Reserve Bordeaux-style reds are the flagship wines at Ravine, but the full-bodied Chardonnay should not be missed. A less costly second label is Sand & Gravel, named after a family business a few generations past.

Winemaker Shauna White and Paul Harber, Ravine Vineyard's chef.

Southbrook Vineyards

Southbrook Vineyards
581 Niagara Stone Road, RR 4
Niagara-on-the-Lake, ON L0S 1J0
(888) 581-1581
(905) 641-2548
southbrook.com

YOU CAN'T MISS Southbrook as you drive down to Niagara-on-the-Lake. You're greeted by a 200-metre-long lavender-coloured wall that hides an immaculately designed winery. For many years, Bill Redelmeier and his wife Marilyn ran a highly successful market garden on their farm — over 115 hectares of lush, rolling countryside between Richmond Hill and Maple, only 24 kilometres north of Toronto. An avid wine collector, Bill then decided to open a winery in his century-old milking barn in 1991. The adjacent milking barn became the barrel-aging room, its massive stone walls thick enough to provide an even, cool temperature all year round. In 2005, after realizing that he really needed to be near his source of grapes, Bill purchased a 30-hectare parcel in the Four Mile Creek sub-appellation that included 14.5 hectares of vines. Then he convinced Ann Sperling to become his director of winemaking and viticulture. Together, they conceived their dream winery, which was given life by Jack Diamond, the designer of Toronto's Four Seasons Centre for the Performing Arts. The reborn Southbrook winery was officially opened on the summer solstice of 2008. Don't be surprised to see sheep grazing among the vines here — Southbrook is a totally organic and biodynamic operation, the first winery in Canada to be certified as such. Winemaker Ann Sperling produces a range of wines of impressive quality, including the Triomphe and Poetica labels and her varietal choice from each vintage under the small-lot Whimsy! label.

Stratus Vineyards

J-L Groulx, Stratus's legendary winemaker.

Stratus Vineyards
2059 Niagara Stone Road
(Regional Road 55)
Niagara-on-the-Lake, ON L0S 1J0
(888) 468-1806
(905) 468-1806
stratuswines.com

STRATUS, THE NEIGHBOURING winery to Jackson-Triggs in Niagara-on-the-Lake, looks like an enormous industrial box store with windows, but it houses the most sophisticated winemaking equipment in the province. Governed by a rigorous Old World winemaking philosophy, the finished wine is a blend of the best barrels, sometimes of different varietals, as in Bordeaux, or different clones of the same grape, as in Burgundy. J-L Groulx, a Loire Valley native who trained in Burgundy and Bordeaux, was the winemaker at Hillebrand Estates for many years before teaming up with vineyard consultant Peter Gamble to design this ultra-modern facility. Both J-L and Peter believe in long hang time for grapes (aided by wind machines in the vineyard to dispel early frosts), dramatically low yields (maximum 2.5 tonnes per acre) and the blending of varietals.

The winery is 100 percent gravity feed for the grapes and the wines to ensure the gentlest handling at all phases of production. Once the wine has finished its journey down to the barrel cellar for aging, it is transported up, for bottling, in steel tanks by means of a central elevator, rather than being pumped up under pressure. Stratus is one of the few Canadian wineries that use large French oak vats rather than stainless steel tanks to ferment the wines. It also believes in long barrel aging. As a result, the wines are some of the best made in Canada. The flagship wines are simply labelled Stratus Red and Stratus White, with the wines not selected for these labels going into a second label wine called Wildass. For instance, the 2008 vintage of Stratus's

Wildass Red was a blend of Cabernet Franc, Cabernet Sauvignon, Merlot, Petit Verdot, Malbec, Gamay, Syrah, Mourvèdre, Tempranillo, Tannat and Sangiovese. The long-aging Stratus White 2007 was a blend of Sauvignon Blanc, Chardonnay, Sémillon, Gewürztraminer and Riesling — all the grapes coming from the winery's own 22-hectare vineyard.

The winery, which opened in 2005, is owned by a group of investors headed by David Feldberg, CEO of Teknion Corporation, a manufacturer of office furniture. The facility is certified LEED — Leadership in Energy and Environmental Design — a North American standard for rating the sustainability of commercial and industrial buildings. A ground loop geothermal system of 25 wells dug 82 metres into the ground uses the earth's energy for all of its heating and cooling needs. Stratus is a winery not to be missed — for its contemporary architecture, its state-of-the-art technology and, above all, its wines and weekly wine and food seminars.

Tawse Winery

Winemaker Paul Pender inspects the vines once the sheep are in bed.

Tawse Winery
3955 Cherry Avenue, RR 1
Vineland, ON L0R 2C0
(905) 562-9500
tawsewinery.ca

FOR THREE YEARS running — 2010, 2011, 2012 — Tawse was voted "Winery of the Year" at *Wine Access* magazine's Canadian Wine Awards, an unprecedented achievement for owner Moray Tawse and winemaker Paul Pender, who joined the team in 2005. Investment banker Moray is a serious Burgundy collector, and when he decided to get into the wine business, he spared no expense in creating an elegant, small-capacity facility with the most modern equipment on the lakeshore plain. The dramatic sloped roof of the contemporary winery, reflected in an ornamental pond, suggests the height within that allows for a gravity-flow operation on six levels, including three barrel-aging cellars.

It was winemaker Deborah Paskus (now at Closson Chase) who convinced Moray to create a winery in Niagara rather than purchase a property in his beloved Burgundy (in fact, he has subsequently purchased Domaine Maume in that region's Gevrey-Chambertin, where Montréaler Pascal Marchand makes wines under the Marchand-Tawse label). A bottle of the legendary Temkin-Paskus Chardonnay (a collaboration between wine writer Steven Temkin and Deborah in the 1990s that produced a few pampered barrels of Burgundy-style white wine) so impressed Moray that he purchased 10 hectares of Beamsville Bench in 2001 and proceeded to build a winery. This acreage included the Vinc Vineyard, containing 25-year-old Chardonnay and 30-year-old Riesling vines. Since then, he

has expanded aggressively, purchasing the 8.5-hectare Cherry Avenue Vineyard (three blocks of which he named after his children, Robyn, Carly and David, each with their own wine — Robyn's Block Chardonnay, Carly's Block Riesling and David's Block Cabernet, respectively). Moray also bought the 3.5-hectare Hillside Vineyard on the Cherry Avenue estate, the 18-hectare Quarry Road Vineyard, the 2.5-hectare Tintern Road Vineyard, the 15-hectare Redstone Vineyard and the 26-hectare Limestone Ridge Vineyard. All are farmed organically or biodynamically. While the primary focus here is on top-flight Chardonnay and Pinot Noir, Tawse also produces Bordeaux varieties, Riesling, Gewürztraminer, Pinot Gris, Sauvignon Blanc, rosé and sparkling wines. In 2012, Tawse produced its first Gamay. A great value series of wines is bottled under the Sketches label. Moray also has vineyard holdings in Argentina.

Thirty Bench Vineyard & Winery

Thirty Bench takes its name from the nearby Thirty Mile Creek on the Beamsville Bench. The winery is housed in a long wooden barn set in the vineyard directly across the road from Angels Gate Winery. The enterprise began as a partnership in the late 1970s — a Riesling-growing operation that, by 1980, had expanded to 15.8 hectares with a whole range of vinifera varietals. In 2005, the Peller family purchased the winery and expanded the property to 23 hectares. Winemaker Emma Garner makes top-flight single-block Rieslings as well as a lusty Bordeaux red blend.

**Thirty Bench
Vineyard & Winery**
4281 Mountainview Road
Beamsville, ON L0R 1B2
(905) 563-1698
thirtybench.com

Vineland Estates Winery

Vineland Estates Winery
3620 Moyer Road
Vineland, ON L0R 2C0
(905) 562-7088
1-888-VINELAND (846-3526)
vineland.com

ONE OF THE handsomest and best-sited wineries in Ontario, Vineland Estates has extensive vineyard holdings that sprawl over 52 hectares. From the facility's large cedar deck, diners can see across the undulating St. Urban Vineyard to Lake Ontario and the Toronto skyline in the distance. Vineland Estates has had several owners since it was founded in 1983, but the Schmidt Brothers, Allan and Brian, have been central to its operation since very early on. Allan, now president, arrived as winemaker and general manager in 1987, while Brian took over responsibility as winemaker in 1994, a role he continues to play in addition to his position as company vice-president.

In 1979, the Mosel wine grower Hermann Weis planted two 20-hectare vineyards to Riesling in Vineland. Using this fruit, Dieter Guttler opened the original Vineland Estates Winery in 1983. Ownership passed to the Weis family five years later, and in 1992, they sold the property to John Howard. He expanded the original winery, preserving the 1845 farmhouse as a tasting room and restaurant, and restored the historic stone carriage house for functions. John also built a new winery with a distinctive stone tower. In 2003, he sold his interest to construction magnate Freddy DeGasperis.

The Schmidts have made Riesling the signature variety here, whether in dry, off-dry, sparkling or Late Harvest and Icewine styles. Vineland Estates has three tiers of wines: the budget-priced Classic Series, which uses machine-harvested fruit; the Elevation Series, under the Niagara Escarpment appellation, produced from hand-picked grapes; and the Reserve Series, made only in the best vintages in limited amounts. Brian Schmidt also

produces the world's first Vodka Icewine Martini, named Vice, and he is excited about the possibilities of Pinot Meunier both as a component in his sparkling wine and as a varietal table wine. The winery's restaurant, a destination on its own, is located in a renovated farmhouse built in 1845 and specializes in local food products that are beautifully prepared. In a barn that dates back to 1877, you'll find the wine boutique, which boasts a magnificent wood bar and an upstairs loft that showcases the original beams. Vineland Estates also offers a Bed and Breakfast cottage and an Estate Guest House on the property.

Winemaker Brian Schmidt, opposite, anticipates a taste of Icewine juice fresh from the press.

Jim Warren
Ontario's Unretiring Wine Advocate

IN 1997, JIM WARREN retired from the halls of academe (he was head of languages at Hamilton's Glendale Secondary School) and made for the vineyards of Niagara. Winemaking had been a basement activity for Jim since his wife Charlotte had given him a winemaking kit in 1970. Three years later, he joined the Amateur Winemakers of Ontario (AWO) and garnered a reputation as one of the best hobbyist winemakers in Canada. While keeping his teaching job, Jim made the leap to professional winemaker in 1984 when Bryce Weylie launched a "juice business" to supply fresh grape juice to amateur winemakers. The following year, in a small barn and garage on the Weylie farm in Stoney Creek, Jim created Stoney Ridge Cellars.

Like its founder, Stoney Ridge has moved around a lot since then. To accommodate a need to expand, Jim partnered with fruit farmer Murray Puddicombe in 1989 and moved the facility to the Puddicombe property in Winona. When that partnership dissolved in 1997 over philosophical differences, Jim found new investors in Ottawa—the Cuesta Corporation—who moved the operation to its present location in Vineland. Barry Katzman and Glen Hunt's company, Wines of Woods End, merged with Stoney Ridge to give it marketing muscle, and eventually, Jim sold his shares to them so that he could concentrate on his burgeoning winemaking responsibilities. He officially retired from the company in 1999, but he still kept his foot in the vat, so to

Icewines produced by students and sold in the campus store at the Niagara College Teaching Winery.

speak, producing the wines for Stoney Ridge's Founder's Signature Collection with his former assistant winemaker Liubomir Popovici. Jim Warren was notorious for the number of wines he would make in a given vintage (one year, he had 62 labels), but notwithstanding this somewhat unconventional approach to commercial winemaking, Jim has garnered an enviable number of awards and accolades over his career.

"In 1999, I was helping Bill Lenko and his son Danny start their winery, and then I received a call from Niagara College," says Jim. "They were planning to develop a Winery and Viticulture Technician program and were interested in interviewing me to help create it. At the same time, I had started my own consulting business and was involved with several other wineries, including Angels Gate, Kacaba, Trillium Hill, Featherstone, Flat Rock and Daniel Lenko. However, I took on Niagara College and started another career there — lucky me! I was also helping some fruit wineries and had started Muskoka Lakes and was beginning to start a winery at Magnetic Hill in Moncton. Looking back, I don't know how it all worked, but most of these people enjoyed a very good start and have become success stories."

Jim Warren may have retired from active winemaking, but he continues to act as executive director of Fruit Wines of Ontario and is involved in advocacy on behalf of the Ontario wine industry. He has completed his first book — *Cellared in Mystery: The Birth of the Ontario Wine Industry* — and is now looking to publish it. "I am also very keen on researching the development of Prohibition and its impact on our wine industry and have started that project," says Jim. "History has once again become an interest in my life."

Colio Estate Wines

Colio Estate Wines
1 Colio Drive, PO Box 372
Harrow, ON N0R 1G0
(800) 265-1322
(519) 738-2241
coliowines.com

IN THE LATE 1970s, the city of Windsor, Ontario, was twinned with the city of Udine in the Friuli-Venezia Guilia wine region in northeastern Italy. A group of local expatriate Friulani businessmen headed by Enzo de Luca, who had grown up with the wines from the region's Collio Hills, decided they could establish a winery in Harrow and replicate the experience. They hired a Friulano winemaker, Carlo Negri, and called their winery Colio (hoping that the name spelled differently would not invoke the ire of their compatriots back home). The company is now owned by Enzo de Luca and Joe Berardo, the proprietor of the Portuguese wine conglomerate Bacalhôa (formerly J.P. Vinhos). At 400,000 cases, it is one of the largest wineries in Canada, with 80 vineyard hectares in the Colchester area of Southwestern Ontario and 8.5 hectares on the Niagara Parkway next to Jackson-Triggs' Delaine Vineyard.

At the end of the 19th century, Lake Erie North Shore was the epicentre of the nascent Canadian wine industry. But when Colio opened in Harrow in 1981, it was awarded the region's first winery licence since Prohibition, giving new life to

Canada's oldest and most historic wine region. Far removed from its major market (a four-hour drive from Toronto), Colio has had to build its consumer base more efficiently than wineries closer to the Golden Horseshoe. It is a commercial winery in the best sense of the word: The owners believe in volume but have maintained creditable quality in their bargain-priced wines. Lawrence Buhler, formerly with Peller Estates, has been making the wines at Colio since 2011. The winery's flagship wines are labelled CEV, while the popularly priced Girls' Night Out and the Lake and River Series appeal to new wine enthusiasts.

With its imposing stone façade, Colio's winery houses over 1.4 million litres of cooperage in both stainless steel and oak. The vast barrel cellar, kept cool and humid by timed sprays of mist, is decorated with two 10-metre-long murals of grape pickers.

Pelee Island Winery

Pelee Island Winery
455 Seacliff Drive
(County Road 20)
Kingsville, ON N9Y 2K5
(800) 597-3533
(519) 733-6551
peleeisland.com

Pelee Island Winery, as part of the Lake Erie North Shore appellation, enjoys three distinctions: It was the site of Canada's first commercial winery, Vin Villa, founded in 1868; it's the only winery that has to ferry its fruit from the vineyard to the winery; and it was the first Ontario winery to produce a commercial quantity of Icewine (Vidal 1983) and the first red Icewine (Lemberger and Blaufränkisch in the 1989 vintage).

In 1980, Austrian winemaker Walter Strehn planted Riesling, Chardonnay and other German varieties on Pelee Island, which at latitude 42° is the most southerly part of Canada, making Pelee Island the warmest appellation in Ontario. Three years later, Walter shipped the grapes back to Kingsville on the mainland for processing. When he returned to his homeland, another Austrian, Walter Schmoranz, took over the winemaking. Today, the winery is one of Canada's largest estates, producing more than 300,000 cases, with grapes sourced from

223 hectares of vines. The wines are made by Martin Janz and Tim Charisse. The facility was built in 1984 and subsequently remodelled. With its white walls and windows defined in local stone, it resembles a prosperous church.

But the real experience is on the island itself, where you will find the Pelee Island Wine Pavilion. From the ferry dock, buses shuttle visitors to the impressive contemporary barn building, approached by a pathway marked by rose bushes. Dominating the interior is a huge wooden wine press from Germany, dated 1723; around it is a museum of winemaking equipment, antique bottles and a photo essay on how corks are made. You can sip the wines on the covered balcony or sit under picnic umbrellas on the expansive grass patio.

The wealth of flora and fauna in the area, with over 10,000 indigenous species of plants and animal life, is celebrated in the variety of the winery's bird and animal labels. Pelee Island showcases some 60 different wines, including eight wines under its flagship Vine-dresser range. The Alvar blends collection is budget-friendly and very well made.

Winemaker Martin Janz.

Sprucewood Shores Estate Winery

Like many operations in Ontario's Essex County, Sprucewood Shores is a true family business. Gordon and Hannah Mitchell planted their vineyard in 1990, selling their grapes to the major producers in Southwestern Ontario. In 2006, they opened their winery, which is a combination of Tuscan and Canadian lakeshore architecture built above two barrel cellars. The facility stands in the 14.2-hectare vineyard, 150 metres from the lake. Tanya Mitchell, Gordon and Hannah's daughter, is a chemical engineer who has taken over the winemaking duties and has a knack for producing rich medal-winning reds.

**Sprucewood Shores
Estate Winery**
7258 County Road 50 West
Harrow, ON N0R 1G0
(866) 938-9253
(519) 738-9253
sprucewoodshores.com

Viewpointe Estate Winery

Viewpointe Estate Winery
151 County Road 50 East
Harrow, ON N0R 1G0
(877) 372-8439
(519) 738-0690
viewpointewinery.com

JOHN FANCSY AND Stephen Fancsy think big. The brothers both gave up lucrative jobs as automobile engineers to start Viewpointe in 2001, and the winery has become something of a showplace for Essex County. They bought into a California vine nursery to supply themselves with their plant needs and currently have 17 different varieties in their three Lake Erie North Shore vineyards. Their gravity-flow facility is a modernistic structure with a stone tower, located right on the bluff of Lake Erie in Harrow. The winery building is connected by an underground barrel cellar to another building in complementary style, which contains a retail store, a commercial kitchen, banquet halls and conference rooms, as well as patios at ground level and on the second floor.

The layout for Viewpointe was inspired by a luxury hotel and resort called the Mettawas Hotel, built in nearby Kingsville by

the legendary distiller Hiram Walker in 1890 and demolished in 1902. The estate itself is made up of three vineyard parcels — Walnut Grove, planted in 2000; Northviewpointe, planted in 2001; and Viewpointe, planted in 1999 and acquired from Sal D'Angelo in 2001 — measuring some 25 hectares in all. The emphasis here is on red wines made from Cabernet Franc, Cabernet Sauvignon and Merlot by John Fancsy. But in addition to its reds, Viewpointe offers a unique white elaborated from rarely cultivated Auxerrois. It offers a very distinct fruit-filled flavour, close to that of Chardonnay, noticeable for its grapefruit and vanilla tone and a long finish.

Closson Chase Vineyards

Seaton McLean in the cellar at Closson Chase.

Closson Chase Vineyards
629 Closson Road
Hillier, ON K0K 2J0
(888) 201-2300
(613) 399-1418
clossonchase.com

THE SEVEN PARTNERS of the new winery — Seaton McLean, Sonja Smits, Andy Thomson, Michael MacMillan, Eugene McBurney, William Fanjoy and winemaker Deborah Paskus — were having a tough time choosing a name. Then it became as clear as the names of the nearest crossroads — Closson and Chase.

The self-contained winery — a building within a building — is housed in a magnificent 1830 double milk barn that has been ingeniously renovated. Sheets of Plexiglas sheathe the interior walls and maintain the integrity of the old structure while ensuring comfort inside. The small vermilion-painted tasting

room, with its tin-sided bar, is an ideal spot to enjoy the only two wines Deborah Paskus makes here — Pinot Noir and Chardonnay. But what wines! Deborah is known for her intense, Burgundian-style Chardonnays and Pinot Noirs, which are produced without compromise from low-tonnage grapes fermented in the best French oak barrels and grown in fractured limestone soil, similar to that found in Burgundy. Before finding a home at Closson Chase, Deborah made wine at Reif (the legendary Temkin-Paskus Chardonnay), 13th Street, Tawse, and Thomas & Vaughan.

Closson Chase's insulated barrel room, a former piggery, is adjacent to the main building and is temperature-controlled by geothermal heating. Though Deborah may profess that Closson Chase is "unsophisticated in terms of technology," the décor, the furniture and the glassware in the tasting room suggest an upmarket wine-bar experience. The winery's evocative labels, inspired by shipping flags, were designed by the renowned Newfoundland artist David Blackwood. The colours are replicated in the stained glass at the main entrance to the winery. In addition to the Chardonnay and Pinot Noir grown on its own 13 hectares, Closson Chase also makes wines from these varietals purchased from growers in the Beamsville Bench and Niagara River sub-appellations of the Niagara Peninsula, as well as a mouth-watering Pinot Noir Rosé. Production is at 2,700 cases — a tiny amount that belies the winery's huge reputation.

The Grange of Prince Edward Vineyards & Estate Winery

The Grange of Prince Edward Vineyards & Estate Winery
990 Closson Road
Hillier, ON K0K 2J0
(866) 792-7712
(613) 399-1048
grangeofprinceedward.com

SOME ARE BORN to wineries, some acquire wineries, and some have wineries thrust upon them. You could say that Caroline Granger belongs to the latter category. In 1972, Caroline's parents, Bay Street lawyer Robert Granger and his wife Diana, purchased a Loyalist farm near Hillier in Prince Edward County. The property, which dates back to 1805, had never been sold, though it had been subdivided by the Trumpour family and used for different purposes over the years. The portion Robert Granger acquired was the site of the home farm, which included the original Trumpour's Mill on Flat Creek. The lumber used to build the magnificent barn that today houses The Grange of Prince Edward's barrel cellar, its tasting room and three other buildings on the property was milled there. The family lovingly restored the 1875 farmhouse, the circa 1826 barn and Trumpour's sawmill and landscaped the grounds around the creek that runs through the property, creating two pond sites. The open-plan tasting room, with its handsome bird's-eye-maple bar and magnificent fieldstone fireplace, is located in the former hayloft and is furnished with local Canadiana pieces. The barrel cellar is located below in the former milking stalls.

In 1997, Caroline, a former Dior model and an actor who had been living in Paris, returned to the farm with her family. In 2001, the Grangers planted the first of five vineyard blocks, which now total 22 hectares. Caroline, having taken a two-year course in vineyard management at Loyalist College in Belleville, was ready to run the family business. She now makes the wines with her daughter Maggie Belcastro. Initially, the winery marketed wines under the Trumpour's Mill label as well as the more upmarket The Grange of Prince Edward label. Now all of their estate-grown wines (6,000 cases) are under The Grange of Prince Edward name. Its traditional method sparkling wine Brut and the Diana's Block Pinot Noir are well worth the search.

Winemaker Adam Delorme at work, above. Caroline Granger, proprietor, opposite, in the barrel cellar.

Hinterland Wine Company

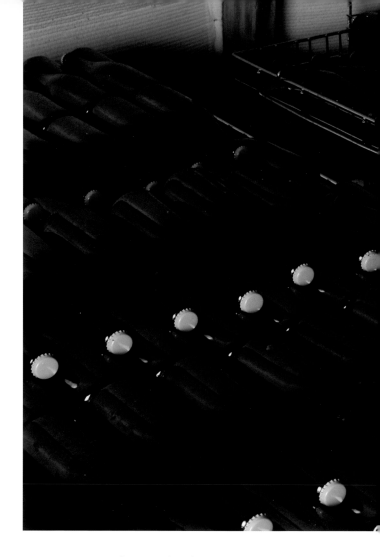

Vicki Samaras with Hinterland's sparkling wines *en tirage.*

Hinterland Wine Company
1258 Closson Road, RR 1
Hillier, ON K0K 1T0
(613) 399-2903
hinterlandwine.com

THE YOUTHFUL OWNERS of Hinterland, Jonas Newman and Vicki Samaras, started their sparkling-wine business in 2007. Jonas came from 15 years in the restaurant business and a two-year apprenticeship at 13th Street Winery in Niagara ("I had Gunther Funk and Herb Jacobson on speed-dial during our first vintages," he says), while Vicki had been interested in owning a vineyard and winery since she was 18. After pursuing an undergraduate degree in biology at the University of Toronto, she developed her skills in sales and marketing while working in the pharmaceutical industry. Like Jonas, she was mentored by the owners of 13th Street, who taught her to grow the best grapes possible.

"Our focus and passion is sparkling wine," says winemaker Jonas, "so much so that we are the only winery in Canada

whose entire production is dedicated to bubbles." Since Hinterland's launch in 2007, Jonas and Vicki have created such a buzz around their products that demand for their 3,200-case production is fierce. They command champagne prices for their Les Etoiles and Rosé, but they also offer a fun wine they've nicknamed "The Babymaker," an off-dry fizzy Gamay labelled Ancestral. To make it, they use an ancient French technique to capture the carbon dioxide gas during the primary fermentation, rather than the Champagne method of a secondary fermentation in bottle. This production method preserves the lightness and fruitiness of the Gamay grape in the wine, which is only 8 percent alcohol.

The winery is housed in a large, free-standing 670-square-metre silver barn adjacent to the couple's 5 hectares of Pinot Noir, Chardonnay, Riesling and Pinot Gris vines. Such is the demand for Hinterland's sparkling wines that Jonas and Vicki have created products using the less costly hybrid Vidal and a tank-fermented (rather than bottle-fermented) bubbly made from a blend of Pinot Gris and Riesling, called Whitecap. For the 2012 vintage, Hinterland produced a charmat method rosé with Cabernet Franc.

Huff Estates Winery

Huff Estates Winery
2274 County Road 1
Bloomfield, ON K0K 1G0
(886) 484-4667
(613) 393-1414
huffestates.com

WHAT MISSION HILL is to the Okanagan, Huff Estate is to Prince Edward County — a go-to winery that, since its opening in 2004, has become a magnet for tourists. The modern industrial building is set back from the road at Huff's Corners (named for Lanny Huff's ancestors, who settled here as United Empire Loyalists). A 4.9-hectare vineyard — one of two owned by Huff that total 14 hectares — leads up to the winery, which sits on top of Mount Pleasant, a high point in the County. Its position allows for a gravity-flow operation to the barrel cellar below.

Lanny is the proverbial local boy made good. A chemical engineer, he made a tidy fortune in the plastics business over 40 years and spent a reputed $6 million to build a state-of-the-art winery with a sunken cellar, advanced technology and a helicopter pad that facilitates corporate getaways to the 20-suite country inn which opened in 2006. A unique winery feature is a free-standing art gallery that exhibits outdoor sculptures as well as works by Canadian artists. The vineyard in front of the winery, once planted to hybrids, is now mostly Pinot Gris and Pinot Noir with a small amount of Vidal.

Huff Estates was the first winery in the region to grow Merlot. To make his wines, Lanny hired the young Burgundy-trained winemaker Frédéric Picard, who has worked vintages in South Africa, Chile, California and Tuscany. In Canada, he has worked with his fellow countryman Jean-Pierre Colas at Peninsula Ridge. Frédéric pioneered the production of sparkling wine in Prince Edward County with his award-winning Cuvée Peter Huff (a wine named to celebrate the life of Lanny's son). In addition to that delicious bubbly, Huff Estates produces top-rated Chardonnay, Pinot Gris and a Merlot/Cabernet Franc blend — 6,000 cases in total.

Julian Huff, owner Lanny Huff's grandson, and sommelier Brian Hanna, opposite, display the winery's latest Chardonnay vintage.

Norman Hardie Winery and Vineyard

**Norman Hardie
Winery and Vineyard**
1152 Greer Road
Wellington, ON K0K 3L0
(613) 399-5297
normanhardie.com

NORMAN HARDIE COULD be making wine in Burgundy or in South Africa. He could be making it in New Zealand or California or Oregon — wherever the siren call of Pinot Noir took him. He has made wine in all these regions. But Norman Hardie chose Prince Edward County. He chose it over Niagara, and he chose it for a very special reason. There was nothing chauvinistic about his decision to stay in Canada and build his winery in Wellington; after all, he was born in South Africa, and he has lived and worked in more countries than you can shake a corkscrew at. It all came down to dirt — a terroir that could support his two favourite varietals, Chardonnay and Pinot Noir.

Norm, as his staff likes to call him, designed the winery in 2004, in collaboration with Ian Starkey, a specialist in rural Ontario architecture. A contemporary New Age barn with a metal roof, redwood-stained pine siding and an underground

Winemaker Norman Hardie.

barrel chamber, the winery melds into the farmscape around it. Talk about living above the shop — Norm resides in a two-storey home connected to the winery by a breezeway.

The building is judiciously situated on a steep slope, allowing for a gravity-flow operation and a barrel chamber to be carved out of the hillside. Remnants of the exposed rock in the cellar show the metre-deep band of solid limestone that runs through the property, an ideal base soil for Pinot Noir. Norm ferments his wines in horizontal milk tanks to ensure that his whites get maximum lees contact for flavour (he stirs the lees of the juice two or three times a day for five days before fermentation to extract maximum flavour), and he gives his reds long skin contact for colour and fine tannin extraction. An appealing feature for visitors is the outdoor wood-burning barbecue and pizza oven he operates during the summer.

The entire Norman Hardie production of 7,000 cases is bottled under screw cap. While Norm specializes in thrilling Burgundian-style Chardonnay and Pinot Noir (his flagship wine is Cuvée L, named for his late sister Lisa) that speak to the County terroir, he also produces Riesling, Pinot Gris, Cabernet Franc and an oyster-designated wine, Melon de Bourgogne (the grape of Muscadet).

Rosehall Run Vineyards

Dan and Lynn Sullivan, owners of a Prince Edward County gem.

Rosehall Run Vineyards
1243 Greer Road, RR 1
Wellington, ON K0K 3L0
(613) 399-1183

D AN SULLIVAN MADE the transition from a highly successful amateur home winemaker to his own commercial winery in 2001. With his partners, Cam Reston and Lynn Sullivan, he bought the picturesque 60-hectare Hillier farm property and named it after a nearby hamlet. The partners chose the vineyard site on Greer Road based on the outstanding Hillier soils and climate: calcareous limestone overlain with stony clay coupled with the moderating influence of Lake Ontario a couple of kilometres to the south — ideal for Burgundian varieties. They planted an initial 6 hectares of vinifera vines, which included 3 hectares to four different clones of Pinot Noir. Now they have just over 9 hectares under vine, featuring such varieties as Ehrenfelser, Gewürztraminer, Sauvignon Blanc and Pinot Gris, and Dan Sullivan's wines are winning awards and accolades nationally and internationally.

Wine-consulting intern Phyllis Wu gets some hands-on experience harvesting grapes in the vineyard.

Dan started off making Rosehall Run wines in a modest barn on the property, but in 2008, he and his partners opened a large new facility that measured 650 square metres and included a barrel cellar blasted several metres deep into the limestone foundation. The space was augmented with a tasting room in 2011. "While retaining the existing vernacular of our farming and grape-growing roots," says Lynn, "we utilized a combination of ultra-eco materials such as cork, Kirei board and straw-fabric veneer. A large three-tiered chandelier was commissioned by local twig artist Maggie Longworth, who fashioned the light using dried grapevines from our property."

Dan's heart, he says, is in Chardonnay, but his Pinot Noirs have won equal acclaim — including a gold medal at the 2011 International Pinot Noir Summit in Napa Valley. In addition to the estate-grown Chardonnays and Pinots, Dan also makes an Alsace-inspired white called Sullyzwicker — a blend of Riesling, Chardonnay, Musqué, Ehrenfelser, Pinot Gris and Muscat Ottonel — and a red under the same label (Cabernet Franc, Gamay, Pinot Noir and Syrah). Rosehall Run, currently producing 5,000 cases, has the distinction of producing the first Syrah grown in the County. The value-priced wines labelled Liberated and Defiant are, respectively, Chardonnay and Pinot Noir.

Icewine

Canada's Gift of Winter to the World

I CEWINE IS ONE of the good things about Canadian winters. Of all the wines made in Canada, Icewine is the wine the world knows best. Within 15 years, this sweet dessert wine has become an international celebrity, an iconic product that is as Canadian as the Mounties, Wayne Gretzky and the maple leaf. Whenever it is entered in competitions anywhere on the planet, Icewine walks off with the medals. It appears on the exclusive wine lists of the world's best restaurants, and you can now buy it in India, Taiwan, Hong Kong, Beijing, New York City, London, Rome and Paris. It's the luxury gift that everyone loves to give and to receive. And like all desirable luxury goods, it is being counterfeited on an unprecedented scale in Southeast Asia. The majority of the phony products end up on wine shelves in Pacific Rim countries. Ontario's Pillitteri Estates is one of the world's largest exporters of Icewine, with nearly 75 percent of its production going to Asian markets. Its exasperated proprietor, Charlie Pillitteri, says: "Imitation is the highest form of flattery, but people are making Icewine in their garage and selling it in China. It's ridiculous."

Fortunately, the Canadian consumer does not have to worry about counterfeit Icewine. If the bottle in the wine store bears a VQA seal, it is the genuine article.

Klaus Reif harvests his Vidal grapes on a frosty December day.

Icewine

KUDOS FOR HAVING produced the first Icewine in Canada go to Walter Hainle, a former textile salesman from Hamburg, Germany, who immigrated to British Columbia in 1970. In 1973, Walter made about 40 litres of Icewine from frozen grapes he had purchased from a local grower in the Okanagan Valley, a tradition he continued until his death in 1995. When he opened his own winery in 1988, one of the first products on the shelf was the 1978 vintage of Okanagan Riesling Icewine. It was not the vinifera Riesling as we know it but, rather, Okanagan Riesling, a fairly insipid grape of dubious origin that was widely planted in the 1960s and 1970s. Since the B.C. vine pullout program of 1989, it has virtually disappeared from the Okanagan.

The very first attempts at producing Icewine on a commercial basis in Ontario were sabotaged by bird and man. In 1983, Inniskillin lost its entire crop to the birds the day before picking was scheduled. That same year, winemaker Walter Strehn at Pelee Island Vineyards, whose vineyard was in the direct flight path of migrating birds from the Point Pelee sanctuary, had taken the precaution of netting his vines to protect them from the feathered frenzy. Some persistent blue jays,

however, managed to break through his nets and were trapped in the mesh. A passing bird fancier reported Walter to the Ministry of Natural Resources, and officials descended on the vineyard and tore off the netting. Walter Strehn not only lost $25,000 worth of Riesling and Vidal grapes to the rapacious flock but was charged with trapping birds out of season and using the dried grapes as bait. Happily, the case was dropped. With the grapes that were left, Walter managed to make 50 cases of Vidal Icewine 1983, which he labelled in the German designation as Beerenauslese Eiswein. He sold the wine to the LCBO (Liquor Control Board of Ontario), which set a retail price of $12.50 a half-bottle. Unfamiliar with this wine style, the consuming public bought very little, and the LCBO returned the majority of bottles and demanded a refund. Pelee Island found a more willing market in the United States, where the product sold for $100 a bottle. The LCBO then begged to have it back.

ICEWINE IS MADE by allowing the grapes to hang on the vine until they freeze naturally. Since the juice is rich in sugar, the temperature has to drop well below freezing and stay there long enough for the bunches to be harvested and pressed while still in their frozen state. A thaw will cause the ice to melt, and the water will dilute the sugars and acids, rendering the juice at harvest below the minimum sugar level of 35 Brix.

A grape berry is roughly 80 percent water. If the berries are frozen solid and then pressed, the water will remain in the skins as shards of ice, allowing small amounts of concentrated juice to flow out. All elements of the juice are concentrated, including flavour, sugar and acidity. The juice from Icewine grapes is about one-fifth the amount you would normally get if you pressed unfrozen grapes. To put it another way, a vine normally produces sufficient grapes to make a bottle of wine, but frozen grapes from a vine produce only one glass of Icewine. Under Canadian wine law, grapes designated for Icewine cannot be picked until the mercury drops to at least minus 8°C for a sustained period of time to allow the berries to freeze, although colder temperatures make for a better-quality Icewine.

The harvesting of Icewine is truly an act of endurance for the pickers: It's usually done in the early-morning hours, before the sun is up. Fermenting the sugar-rich juice in wine can take months, and special hard-working yeast is required. The final alcohol level can vary from 9 to 13 percent, depending on how much residual sugar is left in the wine.

Canadian Icewine first gained global attention at Vinexpo in 1991. Donald Ziraldo and Karl Kaiser, co-founders of Inniskillin Wines, entered their Vidal Icewine 1989 in the biennial wine fair's Challenge Internationale du Vin competition in Bordeaux. Their wine won the Grand Prix d'honneur, one of only 19 such awards for the 4,100 wines submitted by 40 countries. The effect was immediate both at home and abroad. Winemakers in Ontario and British Columbia began to set aside portions of their vineyards for netting to produce Icewine, and overseas buyers began to take a keen interest in the product. Canadian Icewine became an instant cult wine selling for up to $250 a half-bottle in Japan, Taiwan and Hong Kong.

Netted Icewine vines in Niagara College Teaching Winery's vineyard on a winter's day.

Québec

Québec

Canada's Undiscovered Wine Region

I NCREDIBLE AS IT may seem, the growth in the number of Québec wineries in percentage terms is the most significant — and spectacular — in Canada. In 2006, there were 42 producers of wines made from locally grown grapes on under 650 hectares. At the time of writing, there are 87 producers — and more to come.

The impulse for Québecois to make wine must have some ancestral root in their French heritage. Why, an outsider might ask, do they even try? Shut your eyes and think of a vineyard scene: What do you see? Rows of plump clusters of purple grapes nestling in green leaves? The sun beating down from a cloudless sky? Napa Valley? The gentle slopes of Burgundy? Chianti's terra-cotta-tiled hilltop towns?

Now think Québec City, where the mercury can drop to minus 30°C in winter for sustained periods of time. Yet currently, 67 wineries stretch in a large arc from west of Montréal to the Eastern Townships (Cantons-de-l'Est) and to northeast of Québec City. These Québec vintners grow varieties you may never have heard of — Frontenac, Sabrevois, Elmer Swenson 517, Vandal-Cliche and Ste-Croix — grapes that can withstand winter temperatures down to minus 35°C. Nor are the flavour profiles what you may be used to. A wine drinker will probably find these wines lean and tart compared with those of British Columbia and Ontario, but they work well if you carefully select your accompanying dishes.

One of the Québec wine industry's showpieces, Chapelle Ste Agnès features European art pieces and artifacts, opposite, acquired by its owner. Previous spread: Île d'Orléans, the bucolic home of several cider, ice Cider, liqueur and wine producers.

Québec

THE CRADLE OF the Québec wine industry is the Eastern Townships, where, in the early 1980s, l'Orpailleur and Domaine des Côtes d'Ardoise began to press locally grown grapes. A nucleus of some 25 wineries is located here. If you take the epicentre to be the Loyalist town of Dunham in the county of Brome-Missisquoi, this is where it all began. In and around Dunham alone, 20 wineries now produce reds, whites, rosés, fortified wines and Icewine. La Route des Vins runs along chemin Bruce, an ideal way for visitors from both sides of the international border to visit the region's wineries, cideries and fruit growers.

Travel about 100 kilometres east, and you'll find yourself in the basin of Lakes Memphré-magog and Massawipi, one of the largest tourist regions in the Eastern Townships, home to five wineries along La Route des Vins de l'Estrie.

In the 1860s, when Ontario's wine industry became a commercial enterprise with the founding of Vin Villa on Pelee Island, southern Québec already had 30 vineyards sprawling over 40 hectares of land planted to old American hybrids. But these vineyards didn't last long. By the end of the 19th century, the vines had been slowly wiped out by the cold. When Canada started importing inexpensive European wines before and after Prohibition, the effort and expense to keep the vineyards alive was too great. By 1935, only 2 hectares remained in La belle province.

During the 1980s, national pride dictated that Québec should have a wine industry, and today, more than 200 hectares are cultivated in the province's five major growing regions. But while the language may be French and the winemakers look to France for their inspiration, there is nothing conservative and traditional about the way Québec vignerons go about their business. They grow several varieties in their vineyards to determine which will do best in their particular soil and microclimate. And since the grape harvests are small (most are boutique enterprises making a few hundred to a couple of thousand cases a year), they have to blend these different grapes. As a result, you will find wines labelled with proprietary names — Vignoble de Sainte-Pétronille Voile de la Mariée, Vignoble Île de Bacchus Le 1535 or Domaine du Ridge Le Vin du Fouloir — but rarely will you find the grape variety on the label unless it's a Seyval Blanc. Many of these wineries also grow apples for cider as well as grapes for wine. And one product, Iced Apple Wine (Ice Cider), rivals English Canada's Icewine not only in quality but in price as well.

NATURALLY, POLITICS IN Québec is never far from the surface in any enterprise. Québec's winemakers are a highly individual lot, willing to express an opinion about their endeavours when asked — and even when not asked. Two central schools of thought became evident to me during my travels through the province: One school is that Québec should use only Québec-grown grapes. Its advocates have banded together as Vignerons Indépendants du Québec. The other school, L'Association des Vignerons du Québec, believes that growers should plant grapes that are also grown in Ontario, such as Baco Noir and Vidal, the rationale being that if the crop is destroyed during a calamitous winter, winemakers can always buy these varieties in order to have some wine to sell. (These attitudes are not unlike the dual

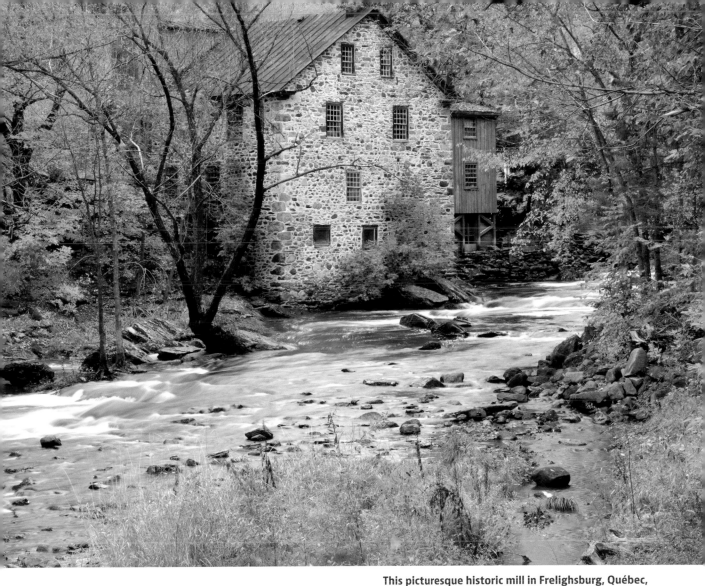

This picturesque historic mill in Frelighsburg, Québec, was built on the Pike River in 1839 by Richard Freligh.

mindset in Ontario's Prince Edward County, where winters are almost as severe.)

But the major problem with Québec wines, according to Gilles Benoît, proprietor of Vignoble des Pins and one of the most progressive of Québec's winemakers, is that his fellow Québecois are not drinking them. "It's the tourists who buy the wines," he says. If that sounds like Ontario 10 years ago, then Québec's future is rosy, because sales will happen thanks to the critical mass of wineries that stimulates growth in agri-tourism.

The charming island estate of Domaine de l'Île Ronde is a short ferry ride across the St. Lawrence River.

O N SEPTEMBER 7, 1535, Jacques Cartier dropped anchor off what he described as "a great island" in the St. Lawrence. There he found masses of wild riparia grapes growing up the trees. Cartier called the island Île de Bacchus, but on reflection — thinking it might be too frivolous a title for his masters in Paris — he renamed it Île d'Orléans as a tribute to Charles, duc d'Orléans, the third son of his monarch, François I.

The Jesuit missionaries who followed in Cartier's footsteps brought with them barrels of sacramental wine, and when they ran out, they tried to make wine by using the native wild grapes. While the wine they produced was tolerable enough to be sipped at mass,

it was not suitable to be quaffed by the early settlers in quantities that would warm their hearts during the long winters in New France.

Voltaire, the French satirist and the embodiment of the 18th-century Enlightenment, referred famously to New France as *quelques arpents de neige* (a few acres of snow), not the most hospitable environment in which to plant vineyards. At that time, New France's upper classes imported their red wine from France or Spain, while the underclass was reduced to brewing a drink from fir branches, which they called "spruce beer."

Québec City is almost on the same latitude

as Burgundy's Côte d'Or, so perhaps the new arrivals dreamed of recreating the wine scenario they remembered from France in their adopted homeland. During the 18th and 19th centuries, they made various attempts to establish a wine industry in Lower Canada, but most were abandoned because of the severity of the climate. However, winemakers are a persistent lot, and by the 1860s, some 30 vineyards south of Montréal covered about 40 hectares. Most of the religious orders had their own plots, thanks to the pioneering efforts of a French nobleman, Count Justin M. de Courtenay, who was convinced that Lower Canada could produce wines that would outperform their Burgundian model.

In 1864, de Courtenay pulled up stakes and moved to Ontario, where he purchased Clair House, the vineyard originally planted by Johann Schiller. But de Courtenay's legacy lived on as other growers struggled to keep their vineyards alive with winter-hardy labrusca varieties imported from the United States. The most notable was the Beaconsfield Vineyard at Pointe Claire, planted in 1877 by a Mr. Menzies, who joined forces with one George Gallagher two years later. But the growing temperance movement had a stifling effect on would-be vintners. Unlike Ontario, where winemaking thrived after the introduction of Prohibition, the vineyards of Québec languished. By the 1930s, only about 2 hectares of vines remained.

The soldiers who returned from Europe in 1945 brought with them a taste for European wine, and the waves of European immigrants who followed had the knowledge and experience to grow grapes and vinify them, if only on a hobby basis. Still, the problem of climate bedevilled postwar efforts in Québec to

Hilling Up: A Vineyard's Winter Coat

The major threat to Québec's vineyards is winter. When the temperature dips below minus 25°C, most buds on French hybrid vines freeze. Growers in what are euphemistically called cool climates, such as Québec and Prince Edward County in Ontario, have devised strategies to protect their vineyards during the bitterest days of winter. Some growers use straw as a cover or plastic sheets tented over the wires. But it is more efficient to protect the buds for next year's shoots by hilling up — lowering the canes on their trellis wires and back-plowing through the rows to throw earth up onto the vines, covering their trunks and lower canes. In the spring, the vines have to be uncovered.

The French oenologist Hervé Durand, one of the founding partners of Vignoble de l'Orpailleur, first used the concept of hilling in Québec in 1982. He had visited vineyards in Russia and China, where he saw farmers bury their vines to protect them against the harsh winters. The vines have to be buried in early November, before the ground freezes, and then uncovered in spring to expose the buds to sunlight. But hilling and unhilling are expensive operations. According to Robert Le Royer of Le Royer St.-Pierre, "burying 16 acres [6.5 hectares] of vines costs us $8,200 for labour and machinery." It is estimated that hilling adds 7 to 10 percent to the cost of a bottle.

The hard-working owner and staff of Vignoble Rivière du Chêne relax at the end of the week.

kick-start a commercial wine industry using homegrown grapes.

Ice can split the trunk of a vine stock, and even the hardiest labrusca varieties are susceptible to winterkill. Most vines can survive temperatures down to minus 25°C, but in Québec, the mercury can drop to as low as minus 30°C. The vine shuts down to protect itself and becomes active only when the temperature finally reaches a consistent 10°C. A certain number of heat units are required during the growing season for grapes to ripen. The total average heat units during this season in Québec is less than 1,000, although certain favoured sites enjoy higher readings because of their microclimates. Iberville,

Québec, gets 1,410 heat units, compared with 1,566 in Vineland in the Niagara Peninsula and 1,629 in Oliver, British Columbia. (By contrast, the Médoc region of Bordeaux has 1,472 heat units; Hawkes Bay, New Zealand, has 1,583; and Napa Valley, California, tops out at a toasty 2,118.)

Québec has highly localized microclimates, especially around Dunham and Magog, which allow the hardier vine stocks to thrive. Topographical features such as large bodies of water or well-protected south-facing slopes offer the grower an opportunity to plant carefully selected varietals. But there is always the problem of winterkill. The most radical measure to safeguard the plants is burial, which protects the buds for the following year's growth. The early settlers in the mid-18th century covered their small acreage of vines with horse manure to protect the plants during the winter, a solution as ineffective as it is impractical today. The process used now is called "hilling" — banking earth over the fruiting spurs and the canes by back-plowing between the rows of vines. However, the newly propagated vines from Minnesota, such as Frontenac, Sabrevois and Louise Swenson, don't require burial.

IN 1980, FRENCH oenologist Hervé Durand purchased a farm in Dunham, Québec, and, two years later, planted a vineyard. His neighbour Frank Furtado was so intrigued that he bought into the dream. Together with winemaker Charles-Henri de Coussergues (and later Pierre Rodrigue), they founded what has become Québec's most successful winery, l'Orpailleur. The enterprise owes its name to the province's renowned singer-poet Gilles Vigneault, who told Durand, "To make wine in Québec is like panning for gold." L'Orpailleur is the French term for a man who searches for gold by panning, an apt metaphor for the time, patience and skill it takes to extract wine from the soil of this province.

The growth and future health of the Québec wine industry will depend on the ability of the wineries to attract tourists. If visitors come, they will buy the wines, enchanted by the historic buildings, the pastoral landscape, the traditional cuisine, the cheese makers, cideries, chocolatiers, bakeries and, above all, the warmth of the welcome. The vintners' pride in their products is infectious, as you will discover when you visit these wineries, each as individual and fascinating as the men and women who work with the grapes in this most difficult of climates.

Wherever there is passion and dedication to grape growing, the potential is there to make fine wines. Québec is a generation behind Ontario and British Columbia in terms of the selection of varieties that are best for its terroir. But as the winemakers discover the best clones to plant and the most effective trellising and pruning methods and allow time for their vines to mature, Québec will produce wines that will astonish you.

After all, it took the Burgundians and Bordelais 200 years to determine what vines flourished best in their soil and climate. In Québec, it will take merely one generation.

Vignoble Rivière du Chêne

Vignoble Rivière du Chêne
807 Rivière N.
St-Eustache, QC J7R 0J5
(450) 491-3997
vignobleriviereduchene.ca

DANIEL LALANDE AND his wife Isabelle Gonthier founded their winery in 1998 on 20 hectares of farmland in the lower Laurentians, close to the 45th parallel. Having assembled an enthusiastic and talented production team for the vineyard and the cellar — which has been under the watchful eye of winemaker Laetitia Huët since 2006 — Daniel and Isabelle have seen their production rise to some 11,500 cases a year, making it a significant player in Québec's wine industry. Laetitia studied viticulture in Beaune, France, the wine capital of Burgundy, and has roots in Val de Loire. A year after her arrival, the enterprise suffered a major setback when a fire completely destroyed the original winery. But disaster turned to triumph with the opening of a brand-new facility in 2008, which boasted a modern tasting room, a banquet room, a gravity-fed tank room and a subterranean barrel cellar. The winemaking equipment in this elegantly designed, multi-level winery is state-of-the-art. A firm believer in wines grown in Québec soil, Daniel says, "Within the framework of the program *Vins du Québec certifiés*, we will ensure that our wines are vinified in the full respect of the climate

and the terroir." Beyond his responsibilities as a winery owner and an advocate for the wines of Québec, Daniel still finds time to play hockey on a local league team.

Ten of the vineyard's twenty hectares are devoted to the production of an Icewine, which is called Monde — a blend of Vidal, Vandal-Cliche and Frontenac Gris. It has found a ready market in China, where 5,000 bottles were shipped in 2012. Monde has won medals in provincial, national and international competitions. Another intriguing product is a fortified red wine blended with maple syrup, called l'Éraportéross. And bubble lovers won't want to miss Rivière du Chêne's semi-dry sparkler, the Monde les Bulles, made by the Champagne method from Vandal-Cliche and Vidal.

Laetitia Huët, winemaker, opposite.
Daniel Lalande, proprietor, right.

Vignoble du Domaine St-Jacques

Vignoble du Domaine St-Jacques
615 Boulevard Édouard VII
St-Jacques-le-Mineur, QC J0J 1Z0
(450) 346-1620
domainest-jacques.com

Yvan Quirion attributes the concentration of his wines to his innovative vine-protection techniques.

YVAN QUIRION GOT the wine bug in his youth while living in the Montréal district of Ville Émard. It happened when he first tasted the homemade red wines of his Italian neighbours. Before plunging himself into the wine business, he studied viticultural practices as if he were working toward a Ph.D. No vigneron in Québec works harder than Yvan Quirion to raise grapes that express the terroir of his 10-hectare vineyard in Saint-Jacques-le-Mineur. He will tell you that his property, a few kilometres from the Richelieu River and the U.S. border, enjoys the same growing conditions in terms of degree days (a measure of heat accumulation between May and September) as Burgundy and the South Island of New Zealand. In 2005, with his wife Nicole Du Temple, Yvan acquired a vineyard of close to 5 hectares that had been planted between 1999 and 2000 to six varieties of hybrids. In 2009, the family planted a 4.9-hectare site in nearby St-Denis-sur-Richelieu to Vidal, Seyval and Maréchal

Foch. Convinced that he could keep the tender vinifera varieties alive during the winter, Yvan planted 8 hectares of Pinot Noir, Pinot Gris, Riesling, Chardonnay and Gewürztraminer on the home site. Rather than hilling the vines in late fall to protect them from winter damage, Yvan uses geotextile fabric as a covering between the rows, a blanketing material that stretches for 32 kilometres across the vineyard. It was his working knowledge of the effects of geotextile that convinced Yvan he could successfully protect a vineyard of vinifera varietals in temperatures that dipped to minus 25°C. Domaine St-Jacques produces blends of hybrids and vinifera. Not to be missed are Yvan Quirion's exquisite red and white Icewines. The winemakers, Frédéric Tremblay and Luc Rolland, produce 350 cases.

Vignoble Le Cep d'Argent

Located between Magog and Sherbrooke, Le Cep d'Argent's vineyard — planted in 1985 by Denis Drouin — slopes down to the banks of Lake Magog. The winemaker at the time, Alain Bayon, introduced Denis to two brothers, sixth-generation winemakers from Champagne named Jean-Paul and François Scieur. The Scieur brothers became Denis' partners in 1991 and were the first to produce a sparkling wine in Québec by the traditional method. Daniel Drouin and the Scieur brothers now run the flourishing company — one of Québec's largest wineries — and its 24 hectares of vines.

Vignoble Le Cep d'Argent
1257, chemin de la Rivière
Magog, QC J1X 3W5
(877) 864-4441
(819) 864-4441
cepdargent.com

Jean-Paul Scieur presents his sparkling wine to guests.

210

Vignoble Chapelle Ste Agnès

Vignoble Chapelle Ste Agnès
2565, chemin Scenic
Sutton, QC J0E 2K0
(450) 538-0303
vindeglace.com

OWNER HENRIETTA ANTONY'S vision was to create an Old World estate in southern Québec. In 1959, she bought 5.5 hectares of land near the village of Glen Sutton, close to the U.S. border, and each time one of her neighbours sold, Henrietta bought the property. She invested millions of dollars to create a Rhône-style vineyard that descends to an ornamental lake and a three-storey stone cellar. But first, she built a gem of a Romanesque chapel consecrated to Sainte Agnès, a 13th-century Bohemian saint. Returning to her native Czech Republic to consult with friends about how to recreate wine cellars worthy of her project, she was taken to the cellars of the Knights Templar, dating back to 1258. And that's what she has recreated here, importing European stonemasons to fashion the cathedral-like chapel, with

Winemaker John Antony, opposite, oversees the production of Icewines and dessert wines in Québec's most impressive winery.

212

its basket-weave vaulted ceilings, medieval arches and stone carvings. "It was done with grey matter. It was done with heart," she will tell you. The 18 terraces of vines that lead up from the artificial lake to the house took four years to build. "I thought they deserved a château," she says, so she had cellars dug into a hillside, on three floors, 13 metres deep. Each of the chambers is furnished with antiques from the 17th and 18th centuries, many of which come from the antique gallery she owns in Montréal. The winery was opened in 1997.

Henrietta's son John is the winemaker, and he produces the most costly wines in the province — nearly all of them sweet dessert wines of international calibre. "This rather singular experience," says John, "is like finding yourself in a late-16th-century castle with a watchtower, a ballroom, a king's suite, multiple underground cellars at four underground levels and an overwhelming number of paintings, carvings, frescoes, Renaissance furniture and suits of armour."

Without question, Chapelle Ste Agnès is Québec's most spectacular winery, and its wines live up to its visual appeal. The 3-hectare amphitheatre-shaped vineyard produces a mere 420 cases of award-winning Icewine, as well as some dry white and rosé wines. Production may be small, but the experience is immense.

Vignoble Clos Saragnat

Vignoble Clos Saragnat
100, chemin Richford
Frelighsburg, QC J0J 1C0
(450) 298-1444
saragnat.com

IN 2003, CHRISTIAN BARTHOMEUF and Louise Dupuis purchased an abandoned 35-hectare apple orchard on the slopes of Mount Pinnacle, a kilometre away from the Vermont border. Some of the trees on the farm were over 70 years old, making it one of the oldest orchards in the province. Drawn to the property because of the number of birds it supported, Christian and Louise suspected that it was a "natural" habitant, unspoiled by fertilizers and other chemicals. Their winery is called Clos Saragnat, after Christian's old family name in his native Arles, in the south of France. Here, near the tiny Loyalist hamlet of Frelighsburg, Christian makes his sweet wines — Vin de Paille, Ice Cider (a category of wine he created in 1989) and Ice Pear.

Volunteer harvester Myriamme Vincent, opposite, happily at work.

Eastern Townships

Christian is a pioneer of the Québec wine industry and its most respected, if controversial, consultant. A strong advocate of organic farming, he rails against the pesticides being used extensively in Québec's vineyards and orchards and claims that pesticides become more concentrated in iced products. He will not even drive a tractor in his vineyard, using his horse Mona Lisa instead to avoid compacting the soil and impeding proper drainage.

Christian cellars his products for three years, without filtration or added sulphites, and he will not use pumps to move the juice or the finished wine for fear of compromising their flavours. As a result, his wines show very clean, concentrated flavours. At under 2 hectares, the vineyard itself is one of the smallest in the province; from it, Christian produces a mere 250 cases.

But the sweet wines that he fashions from his Vidal, Geisenheim, New York Muscat, Petite Arvine and Gamay grapes have won a cult following and have garnered gold medals in competitions around the world. Christian was one of the first recipients of the Governor General's Award in Celebration of the Nation's Table in 2010.

Christian Barthomeuf
Pioneer and Prophet

Clos Saragnat's Christian Barthomeuf and Louise Dupuis.

A SELF-TAUGHT VITICULTURIST AND wine-maker, Christian Barthomeuf was born in Arles, France, in 1951. During a sabbatical from his career in film-making, he came to Québec in 1974, bought a farm in Dunham—and ended up staying. In 1979, Christian planted the first vineyard in Québec's modern era on the property that would become known as Domaine des Côtes d'Ardoise. "When I started planting vines in Dunham in 1979," he says, "I started with a

Adrien Boulicaut and Myriamme Vincent carefully sort grapes destined for Vin de Paille.

a variety of Québec wineries and cideries. Notable among them are Domaine des Côtes d'Ardoise, in Dunham, where he made Canada's first Ice Cider in 1989; La Face Cachée; Domaine Pinnacle; and Chapelle Ste Agnès. Christian was also the first to produce a sparkling Ice Cider.

Twenty-five years ago, Christian will tell you, he believed he could make wine in Québec. Today, he says, "Wine is an international business. I don't think that Québec could easily compete against any wine product elaborated abroad with a good quality-price ratio, with the exception of Icewine and Vin de Paille. As a winemaker, I started my career in Québec with dry white and red wines. I quickly realized that our climate and production costs would make it hard to really compete with major exporters such as Chile, Argentina, Italy, California and Australia."

As a result, Christian is aiming at a different market altogether. At Clos Saragnat, the property he and his partner Louise Dupuis bought in 2002, he has concentrated his efforts on high-level, high-priced products that appeal to the international market — Vin de Paille, Icewine and Ice Cider. No pesticides or herbicides are used here, and the wines see no added sulphites. Together, Christian and Louise run the vineyard and the orchard using rigorous sustainable practices, doing vineyard work with horses rather than tractors and using electric carts rather than fossil-fuel-powered vehicles on the property.

book in my hand. The same thing for wine. I can cook. The rest is feeling." Eventually, Christian sold Domaine des Côtes d'Ardoise to Montréal plastic surgeon Jacques Papillon, and in 2010, Jacques in turn sold the property to Steve Ringuet and his group of investors.

Based on the experience and reputation Christian earned during those pioneering days in the 1980s, he began consulting to

Vignoble Domaine du Ridge

Vignoble Domaine du Ridge
205, chemin Ridge
Saint-Armand, QC J0J 1T0
(450) 248-3987
domaineduridge.com

I N THE SPRING of 1996, Denis Paradis, then a federal Liberal Member of Parliament, planted 2,000 Seyval Blanc vines on his farm in St. Armand, a property that extended over 17 hectares. Three years later, he opened his winery. Today, the vine count is 55,000, making Domaine du Ridge one of the most important wineries in the province.

Denis will tell you candidly that he knew nothing about wine production until one of his neighbours, a European, convinced him to plant a vineyard and offered to teach him how to make wine. The approach to the winery is through a majestic, over-arching tunnel of ancient maple trees. The Loyalist Victorian

Proprietor Denis Paradis in his tank cellar.

house on a sequestered side road is now the winery office. The heavy lifting is done by winemakers Jean Berthelot and Julian Torchut in a new barn designed to meld with its pastoral setting. The time to visit this winery is during harvest, especially for an event Denis calls "Cuvée du Fouloir," when 20 women are invited to foot-crush his Seyval Blanc to musical accompaniment. (According to Denis, the activity honours a medieval tradition where only female virgins were allowed to perform this function.) The crushing tank for the enterprise looks like an outdoor Portuguese port lagar — but it's actually the base of an old silo that Denis had restored and remodelled with oak panelling.

A walk through the 81-hectare property under tree-lined paths is a delight in the summer heat. But the foot-crushing of the Seyval Blanc is the real show. Production is now at 8,000 cases. The winery's most successful products are a dry rosé made from Seyval Noir and a Late Harvest Seyval Blanc called Brise d'Automne. You can sit on the terrace in summer and fall and indulge in a little pétanque if you're feeling *sportif*.

Domaine Les Brome

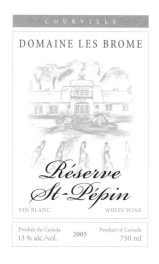

Domaine Les Brome
285, chemin Brome
Ville de Lac Brome, QC J0E 1S0
(450) 242-2665
domainelesbrome.com

A FORMER PRESIDENT AND CEO of the National Bank, Léon Courville's passion for wine dates back to the early 1970s when he was in the United States studying for his Ph.D. in economics. When it was still affordable to do so, he began collecting the great wines of the world, and he has maintained his collection ever since.

Léon acquired the Lac Brome property as a family retreat in 1981. In 1999, he planted an experimental vineyard on the property, and today, that has grown to 14 hectares. Running down to Lac Brome, the vineyard is planted to 12 varieties — Vidal, Geisenheim, Seyval Blanc, Seyval Noir, Riesling, Chardonnay,

St-Pépin, Maréchal Foch, De Chaunac, Pinot Noir, Baco Noir and Cabernet Franc. In addition to pursuing their passion for wine, Léon and his wife Anne-Marie Lemire raise Salers cattle and produce a high-grade maple syrup.

The initial winery was established in 2000, but as production increased, operations had to be moved to an old sugar shack, which was expanded to accommodate square stackable fermentation vats — a space-saving device, as cylindrical tanks take up more room. The

The Domaine Les Brome vineyard features a reproduction of a painting by Gilles Carle, the late Québécois filmmaker and visual artist, titled *Que vient faire cette picassienne dans ma toile ?* Viticulturist Henry-Alain Drocourt with a local worker, opposite.

timber used in the construction of the fermenting cellar and wine shop was felled from the forests surrounding the vineyards in order to maintain the environmental integrity of the site.

In 2005, the new winery was opened to the public. Two Burgundy-trained winemakers preside over the cellar: Jean-Paul Martin, the proprietor of Grange Hatley, and Amélie Oustau, a master of oenology from Dijon. Domaine Les Brome is renowned for its St-Pépin; in fact, it is the first winery in Québec to produce commercial quantities of this winter-hardy grape propagated by the University of Minnesota. Other products that have captured the attention of critics and wine lovers alike are the Vidal Réserve, the Cuvée Charlotte and a unique Vidal Icewine aged in French and American oak barrels. The winery produces about 3,000 cases.

Vignoble de l'Orpailleur

Vignoble de l'Orpailleur
1086, route 202 (rue Bruce)
Dunham, QC J0E 1M0
(450) 295-2763
orpailleur.ca

IN 1982, TWO French winemakers, Hervé Durand and Charles-Henri de Coussergues, along with a Québec associate, theatrical producer Frank Furtado, planted a vineyard in Dunham. Their winery was to be called Vignoble du Château Blanc, after the property's historic farmhouse. Three years later, they took in another partner, Pierre Rodrigue. Thanks to a poem composed by Gilles Vigneault, in which he likened growing wine in Québec to panning for gold, the enterprise was renamed l'Orpailleur (the gold panner). The name also tips its hat to the number of gold-bearing rivers in the Cantons-de-l'Est. The original wood house, an hour's drive from Montréal, has been expanded in colonial style to include a restaurant called Le Tire-Bouchon and a wine shop. From the building's lookout tower on the second floor, you can see a commanding view of the surrounding vineyards, of which l'Orpailleur owns close to 23 hectares. Here, Charles-Henri introduced the northern European and Russian practice

of "hilling" vines (covering them with soil to protect them through the winter months and then uncovering them in the spring).

Inside, l'Orpailleur's original house — a former inn — is an exhibit of wine culture through the ages, complete with a collection of antique corkscrews. If you visit only one winery in Dunham, this one will give you the complete Québec wine experience and a history lesson to boot — the hour-long tour includes a video. In September, l'Orpailleur sets off fireworks to mark the beginning of the grape harvest — courtesy of Frank Furtado, who puts on firework displays across Canada. Charles-Henri was the original winemaker, but those duties now are undertaken by Marc Grau, who immigrated to Québec from the south of France in 1991 and joined the winery in 2005. His oak-aged Seyval Blanc is one of the best I've tasted. Other wines worth seeking out are Vin de Glace and La Part des Anges. With its production of 15,000 cases, l'Orpailleur is the largest winery in the province.

Charles-Henri is currently the president of the influential L'Association des Vignerons du Québec. As its leading spokesman, he lobbies his peers in the industry, the wine-loving public and elected politicians to hammer home the message that Québec's winemakers can and do produce wines of quality. And through it all, he remains a humble and welcoming champion of the wines of his adopted country.

Vignoble Sainte-Pétronille

Proprietor Louis Denault with his guest Hélène.

Vignoble Sainte-Pétronille
1A, chemin du Bout-de-l'Île
Ste-Pétronille, QC G0A 4C0
(418) 828 9554
vignobleorleans.com

LOUIS DENAULT AND Nathalie Lane's winery sits high above the St. Lawrence at the western end of Île d'Orléans, with a magnificent view of the river, Montmorency Falls and the graceful bridge to the island. The roughly 5 hectares of vineyards that slope down to the banks of the St. Lawrence are bordered by large mature stands of sugar maples and American oak, which provide magnificent colours in the fall season. Here you will find the first commercial planting of the renowned grape breeder Joseph Vandal's newly developed crossing, Vandal-Cliche, the first hybrid that did not need winter protection. This grape is widely planted in the province (10 wineries currently use it), and it produces a white wine with a fruity, almost grapey character. If you want to witness some oenological history, make a beeline for Sainte-Pétronille itself to see where the previous owner, Jean Larsen, planted the first commercial Vandal-Cliche vineyard in 1990. At Sainte-Pétronille, it finds its best expression in a wine called La Voile de la Mariée (blended with Vidal).

The winery is in the basement of an elegant Normandy-style house, with a green roof and large covered verandahs. While it looks as though it has been there for two centuries, it was built in 1991 by owners Louis Denault and Nathalie Lane. Winemaking is a second career for Louis, who once built bridges as well as other major construction projects. Now his building is restricted to his property, where he added the shop, tasting room and bistro in 2006. The couple make seven wines here, including a Riesling, a Late Harvest Riesling and a Mistelle called Insula (Vandal-Cliche fortified with brandy). Production is 3,500 cases. The view from the vineyard and the winery alone are worth the visit. Looking toward Montmorency Falls, especially from the terrace, is a photographer's dream.

Ice Cider

Québec's Winter Wine

GIVEN QUÉBEC'S WINTER climate and the province's abundance of apple orchards, it's only natural that Ice Cider should be to La belle province what Icewine is to Ontario. First produced in 1990 by Christian Barthomeuf, it is now made by some 50 producers across the province. In fact, Québec makes almost as much cider as it does wine. It's a cottage industry whose history stretches back to the 17th century and the first settlers in the province from Normandy and Brittany. Those early pioneers brought cider with them but soon found that the conditions around Montérégie (between Montréal and the U.S. border) were ideal for growing apples. As a result, cider-making has been a venerable and venerated occupation in Québec. Today, the range of styles is impressive — from dry to sweet and sparkling to fortified. But none is more cherished than Ice Cider.

Of all Québec's wines, Ice Cider is perhaps the one that will become an iconic product internationally, just as Icewine has become for Ontario, British Columbia and Nova Scotia. What is Ice Cider? Think of Icewine, and replace the frozen grapes with frozen apple juice. You get the same honeyed sweetness and racy acidity in Ice Cider as you do in Icewine. But it tastes of apples, of course, rather than the more concentrated peach and tropical fruit flavours found in Icewine.

Ice Cider tasting during the *Fête des vendanges de Magog-Orford*, above. Camille Nantais-Martin and François Duquette, opposite, share an Ice Cider toast in the orchard of Domaine Pinnacle.

Allegedly once owned by Prohibition-era rum-runners, Domaine Pinnacle's 1859 farmhouse is said to have done service as a Québec-Vermont border lookout.

While grapes for Icewine have to be frozen naturally on the vine as stipulated by the VQA, the apples for Ice Cider can either be picked after the first autumn frost or left to freeze on the tree and then harvested and pressed. There are two schools of thought here. At La Face Cachée de la Pomme, Québec's leading ciderie, both styles of Ice Cider are made: Neige, by freezing the pressed juice — a process that separates much of the water in the juice as ice, which, when removed, leaves a highly concentrated, syrupy liquid ready to be fermented; and Frimas, by pressing frozen apples that have been left to hang until winter's end. The product label tells you which technique was used. The other leading producer, Domaine Pinnacle, blends its Ice Cider with apple brandy to make a product called Réserve 1859.

Christian Barthomeuf, who created the original Ice Cider in 1989 at Domaine Pinnacle (he makes the product for his own winery and three other producers), favours the tree-frozen method. "I make 90 percent of my production this way because the result is definitely better. It is almost like Icewine." For the other 10 percent, Christian leaves the juice to freeze outdoors and adds pear juice to the mix.

Jean-Guy Gosselin, at Côteau St-Paul, also believes you make a better product if you leave the apples on the trees until they are completely frozen and then pressed in their frozen state.

As with Icewine, regulations prohibit the use of industrial freezers for either the apples or the extracted juice. According to the organization Cidriculteurs artisans du Québec, the natural sugar in the juice to be fermented must measure at least 310 grams per litre, and no other sweetener can be added. Nor can the producer add alcohol if it is to be sold as Ice Cider. Fermentation can take as long as seven months or more. After fermentation, the residual sugar in the wine must be at least 150 grams per litre, with an alcohol level between 9 and 13 percent, depending on the style produced. It can take as much as 7 kilograms of apples to make one 500-millilitre bottle of Ice Cider.

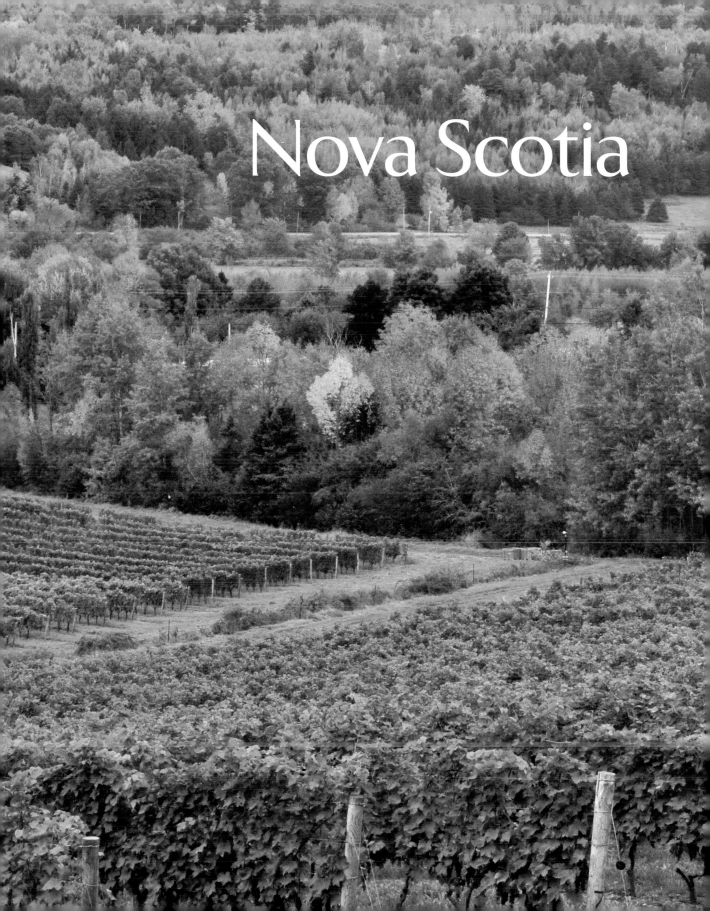

Nova Scotia

Nova Scotia

and the Atlantic Provinces

THERE ARE CURRENTLY 17 wineries in Nova Scotia, 14 in New Brunswick, four in Newfoundland and Labrador and two on Prince Edward Island. The coming of age of the Nova Scotia wine industry was signalled on June 12, 2012, when the Winery Association of Nova Scotia unveiled its own provincial appellation: Tidal Bay, a crisp white wine made from 100 percent locally grown grapes. In that inaugural vintage, 10 wineries made a wine according to its regulations.

It might seem fanciful to think of the Atlantic provinces as a wine-growing region. Most people "from away" have an image of icebergs, howling gales, raging seas and pitiless snowbound winters. But nature has a way of compensating climate-challenged regions with oases of calm and relative tranquility. It may surprise you to learn that St. John's, Newfoundland, is Canada's third-warmest city in winter, ranking just below Victoria and Vancouver in mean temperature. Look at a map, and you will see that most of the Maritime provinces are located farther south than British Columbia.

Glenda Baker's Dark Cove Winery at Gambo, 40 kilometres east of Gander, Newfoundland, has 31 grape varieties planted in its vineyard, including such tender vinifera varietals as Chardonnay, Gewürztraminer and Pinot Noir. Glenda will tell you that roses, irises, Saskatoon berries, blueberries, bilberries, cherry trees and apple trees grow wild there. "From all indications, Gambo appears to be well suited for cool-climate viticulture," she says, "in spite of the fact that it's on the same latitude as Paris, France, and Volgograd, Russia."

Wolfville's Blomidon Inn, opposite, was built at the end of the 19th century as a private residence. The lush Gaspereau Valley, previous spread, is home to Gaspereau Vineyards.

Nova Scotia

Nor should we forget that in AD 1001, when Leif Ericson set sail from Norway in a Viking longboat, he eventually landed at L'Anse aux Meadows in northern Newfoundland. Noting the proliferation of wild grapes, he named the place "Vinland." This legend had its echo over 500 years later, when Jacques Cartier found an abundance of wild grapes growing on an island in the St. Lawrence and named it Île de Bacchus.

The fact that there are not more wineries in the Atlantic provinces should be the surprise, given that the urge to make wine has, over the past 20 years or so, become a passionate pursuit of many Canadians. Even armchair vintners dream of retiring to a grape-growing region and planting a vineyard.

MIDWAY BETWEEN THE equator and the North Pole, Nova Scotia may seem an unlikely wine-growing region, but wine growers and local consumers are fiercely proud of their homegrown wines. Wherever you go, you will find the local wines displayed on lists in hotels as elegant as the Blomidon Inn in Wolfville (a *Wine Spectator* magazine Grand Award winner) and in the smallest guest houses along the Evangeline Trail.

Nova Scotia has a legitimate claim as the site of the first vineyard planted in Canada. In his *History of New France*, Marc Lescarbot, a French lawyer and historian, chronicled the year he spent at Port Royal in 1606–07. Lescarbot wanted to be Nova Scotia's first vigneron, but he was frustrated in this enterprise by a forgetful shipmate. He writes of his discovery of grapevines while exploring the coast near the Saint John River in New Brunswick with Jean de Biencourt, Seigneur de Poutrincourt: "The said M. de Poutrincourt

seeing there such excellent grapes gave orders to his valet to tie up and put in the long-boat a bundle of vines they had taken. Master Louis Hébert, our apothecary, who wished to dwell in these parts, had rooted a large number of them, with the intention of planting them at Port Royal, where there are none, though the soil there is well fitted for vines; but this was

Harvest week at Gaspereau Vineyards.

stupidly forgotten and neglected to the great displeasure of the aforesaid gentleman and of us all."

The desire of the French settlers to plant vineyards was eventually satisfied in the spring of 1633, when the high-ranking naval officer Isaac de Razilly, chosen by Cardinal Richelieu to reclaim Acadia for France, set up

241

the French outpost Fort-Ste-Marie-de-Grace (now LaHave, once the capital of Acadia/ Nova Scotia). In the following year, de Razilly wrote to Marc Lescarbot, who had returned to France: "I have planted some vines as they do in Bordeaux which come along very well.... Vines grow here naturally. The wine made from these has been used to celebrate mass." Unfortunately, de Razilly never did get to enjoy the fruit of the vineyard he cultivated, because he died suddenly in December 1635.

With the expulsion of the Acadians in 1755, grape growing for the production of wine in the province came to an end and would not be revived until the second half of the 20th century. In *The Tangled Vine: Winegrowing in Nova Scotia*, Chris Naugler writes: "However, table grape growing was still a promising occupation. The first reference to viticulture by English settlers comes from the early 1800s when Charles Prescott imported and grew Isabella grapes on his farm at Starr's Point in the eastern Annapolis Valley." (Isabella, the North American hybrid noted for its resistance to powdery mildew, would become the carrier of the phylloxera louse that laid waste the vineyards of Europe in the 1870s — a vine plague whose damage was estimated at two and a half times the total cost of the Franco-Prussian War.)

By the mid-19th century, commercial production of table grapes thrived on family farms in the Annapolis Valley and along the South Shore. The province's first commercial winery to use locally grown grapes was created by Roger Dial, a political science professor at Dalhousie, in 1980. Roger, a Californian, had trained as a winemaker at David Bynum in Sonoma and had planted experimental vineyards in the Annapolis Valley as early as 1977. He called his enterprise Grand Pré Wines. Among other hybrids in the vineyard that Dr. Norman Morse, Roger Dial's partner in the winery, planted were two Russian red varieties, Michurinetz and Severnyi. These unusual grapes had arrived at the Agriculture Research Station in Kentville via a circuitous route.

Unfortunately, Roger's vision outstripped his finances, and in 1987, with a plunging stock market, he was forced to close the doors on his cottage winery. But after a lengthy reconstruction, they would open again in spectacular fashion — under the proprietorship of a Swiss banker Hanspeter Stutz — as the grandly named Domaine de Grand Pré.

The wines produced here, given that climate, are high in acidity. Chardonnay is a rare commodity in Nova Scotia, but the locally propagated L'Acadie Blanc can be made in Chablis style, as crisp and dry as a Granny Smith apple. Seyval Blanc, once an important white grape in Ontario and now out of favour, is widely planted here, delivering a crisp, citrusy wine with racy acidity. Another Nova Scotia specialty is New York Muscat, which, with its aromatic bouquet and flavours of orange blossom and cardamom, is ideal for spicy dishes. While efforts are being made to grow Pinot Noir, the most successful red variety is the hybrid Maréchal Foch, which makes a wine with a sour cherry flavour not dissimilar to Beaujolais. Arguably, of all Canada's regions, Nova Scotia's wines are most in tune with its regional dishes, which feature fish and seafood and locally grown vegetables.

For all the difficulties it faces as a wine-producing region, the enthusiasm and confidence of the winemakers about the future of their

Katie Barbour, winery manager at Gaspereau Vineyards (centre) with friends Ceileigh and Adan.

enterprise are infectious. (Nearly everyone connected with the industry has a car licence plate that reads NS WINE.) An industry-developed study in 2002 projected that, by 2020, Nova Scotia will have 20 wineries. The authors describe the Annapolis Valley as similar to Germany's Rhine Valley, and the Gaspereau Valley as akin to the Mosel. If Ontario is like Bordeaux and Burgundy in its growing season, then this comparison is fairly apt.

Given the number of wine growers who currently sell their grapes to the existing wineries — and a surprisingly high number of these growers are either doctors or dentists — the goal of 20 wineries will most likely be reached and surpassed before 2020. Grape growers typically get the itch to see their name on a wine label, and that means opening their own winery.

Since sparkling wines require grapes that are not as ripe as those needed for table wine, this region is ideal for the production of champagne-style bubblies — and that's exactly what Benjamin Bridge and L'Acadie Vineyards in the Gaspereau Valley are showing the world.

Domaine de Grand Pré

Domaine de Grand Pré
11611 Highway 1, PO Box 105
Grand Pré, NS B0P 1M0
(866) GP WINES · 866-479-4637
(902) 542-1753
grandprewines.ns.ca

Hanspeter Stutz, a Swiss banker, bought Roger Dial's old Grand Pré winery from the next owners, Jim Landry and Karen Avery, in 1996. Founded in 1978, the winery might have the right to claim to be the oldest in the province — except that Hanspeter closed it down for the next four years while he spent several million dollars replanting the vineyards and constructing a showplace winery and cellar. Part of the beautifully landscaped site — with its cobblestoned walkways inlaid with giant grape leaves of granite, it's like a small, very tidy and elegant wine hamlet — is an art gallery below the tasting room and a cottage-style restaurant with a Swiss menu called Le Caveau. From the art gallery, you have a view into the wine cellar. During the recon- struction, Hanspeter sent his son Jürg to the Waedenswil wine school in Switzerland to learn winemaking. Three years later, Jürg returned for his first crush in 1999. "We want to make wine with 100 percent Nova Scotia-grown fruit," he said at

that time. "Something I'm really aiming for is the clean, crisp wines you get in Switzerland."

Hanspeter reopened the dazzling complex as Domaine de Grand Pré in 2000. Since then, it has become a magnet for tourists. Although the winery is based mainly on hybrid varieties grown on 12 hectares, Hanspeter has an experimental mother block with 44 varietals. The pergola is an ideal spot to sit with a glass of wine and take in the luxurious feeling of the place. Hanspeter also makes sparkling fruit wines and an excellent cider; one has the sense that he is as proud of his cider as he is of the wines his son makes. The attractive art labels, the ultra-modern tasting-room bar and the carved stone inlays in the cellar make this winery a distinctive one to visit.

Winemaker Jürg Stutz and his wife Cäcilia Stutz-Spirig, above. Jürg and Hanspeter Stutz, proprietor, top.

L'Acadie Vineyards

L'Acadie Vineyards
310 Slayter Road, RR 1
Wolfville, NS B4P 2R1
(902) 542-8463
lacadievineyards.ca

I N 2004, WHEN Bruce Ewert moved from British Columbia (specifically from Summerhill Pyramid Winery) to Nova Scotia, he brought a wealth of experience in the production of sparkling wines. That his wife Pauline Scott was born in the province no doubt had something to do with the decision to move across the country, but Bruce, whose training in sparkling-wine production includes vintages in California, Australia and Ontario, also believed the climate and soils of the Gaspereau Valley to be ideal for traditionally made bubblies.

As the name of the winery suggests, the emphasis here is on the L'Acadie grape. As Nova Scotia's most widely planted grape, L'Acadie is unique to the province, apart from small plantings in New Brunswick. Although it was bred in 1953 by O.A. Bradt in Ontario's Horticultural Research Institute at Vineland Station,

it never caught on with Niagara growers. A winter-hardy, early-ripening grape, L'Acadie is perfect for short growing seasons. It's a cross of Cascade x SV14-287 and can survive in temperatures down to minus 31°C. Since the winery's founding, L'Acadie Vineyards has been a totally organic operation both in the 4-hectare vineyard and in the fermenting cellar. In addition to the vintage-dated sparkling wines, white and rosé, Bruce also makes cider, a still L'Acadie, two reds using the grape-drying process of appassimento, a Nouveau of Maréchal Foch and a dessert wine called Estate Soleil using the same method. L'Acadie Vineyards produces about 2,000 cases.

Maritimer Pauline Scott and husband Bruce Ewert, top, owners of L'Acadie Vineyards.

Benjamin Bridge Vineyards

Benjamin Bridge Vineyards
1842 White Rock Road, RR 1
Wolfville, NS B4P 2R1
(902) 542-1560
benjaminbridge.com

THIS WINERY IN the Gaspereau Valley is making waves not only in Nova Scotia but in the international wine world as well. The quality of its sparkling wines is such that proprietor Gerry McConnell has the chutzpah to mount blind tastings of his products against the finest champagnes of France—and with gratifying results. In keeping with the new wave of Canadian wineries, Benjamin Bridge's owner made his fortune in another field (mining) before getting his feet into the vat, so to speak. In 1999, he purchased a 20-hectare farm property with an 1845 Westcott family barn and did an initial vineyard planting of 4 hectares (now augmented by another 13 hectares). Gerry hired Peter Gamble as lead consultant on the project, and taking into account Nova Scotia's climate, they wisely decided to concentrate on sparkling wines. They set their sights ambitiously high: Gerry

wanted to make sparkling wine up to the standard of the Champagne region's prestige cuvées. Peter, the original winemaker at Hillebrand, suggested that if you want to rival great champagne, you have to get a top Champenois winemaker to consult — which is exactly what Gerry did. Oenologist Raphael Brisbois has worked at Piper-Heidsieck, Omar Khayyam in India, Mountain Dome in Washington and Blue Mountain in British Columbia.

Peter and Raphael have been experimenting with sparkling blends since 2002, using Pinot Noir, Chardonnay, Vidal and Nova Scotia's signature white grape L'Acadie. Jean-Benoit Deslauriers joined the team as resident winemaker in 2008. Today, the sparkling wines are made only with the traditional vinifera grapes — Chardonnay, Pinot Noir and Pinot Meunier. Gerry McConnell has given them carte blanche to leave the wines on the lees as long as they want. The results are astonishing. They are, without question, the best sparkling wines I have tasted in Canada. In addition to the fine — and costly — bubblies, Benjamin Bridge also produces a delicious Muscato-like sparkling wine called Nova 7, an Icewine called Borealis, Nexus Rosé, a Maréchal Foch called Taurus and a Tidal Bay blend called Vero.

Gaspereau Vineyards

Gina Haverstock, winemaker.

Gaspereau Vineyards
2239 White Rock Road
Gaspereau, NS B4P 2R1
(902) 542-1455
gaspereauwine.com

WINEMAKER GINA HAVERSTOCK presides over a cellar that produces top-flight Rieslings as well as a series of three traditionally made sparkling wines (Pinot Noir, Chardonnay and Riesling), a delicious dry Muscat, a red hybrid Lucie Kuhlmann and an unusual Icewine made from Ortega and Vidal grapes. When Hans Christian Jost purchased the property and planted the vineyard in 1996, his intention was to create Nova Scotia's smallest winery, topping off at 2,000 cases (he already owned the province's largest winery, Jost Vineyards in Malagash). But as the popularity of Gaspereau Vineyards' wines grew, so, too, did its production, which is currently over 4,000 cases. Hans Christian planted his vineyard on a 200-year-old apple orchard and built a small red barn winery in the Gaspereau Valley because he believed the valley has the greatest potential of

any area in Nova Scotia for growing grapes and marketing wine. And he seems to have been proven correct in his vision. The soil here varies markedly between the lower south-facing slope nearer the winery, consisting of loam (and planted to L'Acadie, New York Muscat, Seyval and Lucie Kuhlmann), and the warmer upper part that is mainly clay loam and slate (good for Chardonnay, Riesling and Vidal). In 2012, Gaspereau Vineyards and Jost Vineyards were acquired by Atlantic Canadians Carl and Donna Sparkes. Their vision is to create great Nova Scotia wine brands and establish markets across Canada and beyond. Hans Christian Jost continues to play a key operational role in both enterprises.

Jost Vineyards

Jost Vineyards
48 Vintage Lane
Malagash, NS B0K 1E0
(800) 565-4567
(902) 257-2636
jostwine.com

WHEN CARL AND Donna Sparkes took control of Jost Vineyards in 2012, they acquired Nova Scotia's biggest and longest-established winery, boasting a 55,000-case production. They also inherited the enormous good will that the Jost family had built up since planting their first vineyard on the Malagash Peninsula nearly 35 years ago. Jost markets 42 different products. It would take you six weeks at a bottle a night to try them all. Thanks to Hans Christian Jost's tireless efforts in promoting his grape wines, fruit wines and specialty wines, he manages to sell them all and, at the same time, beat the drum for Nova Scotia wines.

Hans Christian, as everyone calls him, farms 18 hectares of vines that date back to 1978, when his father Hans Wilhelm and his wife Erna established the vineyard on the Malagash Peninsula overlooking the Northumberland Strait. The company has an additional 52.5 vineyard hectares under contract throughout the province. (Hans Christian is fond of saying that you could fit the entire grape acreage of Ontario into the Malagash Peninsula, and there would still be lots of vineyard land available.)

After completing courses for a diploma in business, Hans Christian went to Germany in 1985 to study viticulture and oenology under the renowned professor Helmut Becker at the Research Centre Geisenheim. A year later, Jost Vineyards received its farm winery licence. In 1988, following the death of his father, Hans Christian was thrust into the position of

Proprietors Donna and Carl Sparkes.

Malagash Peninsula

Winemaker Chris Frey.

running the family winery at a young age. Since then, he has become the unofficial leader of Nova Scotia's nascent wine industry. His colleague, Chris Naugler, says of him: "In his kind, soft-spoken way, he has been a cheerleader for the whole industry here. Most important, he has been a strong advocate of single vineyard bottlings, which has allowed us to begin examining the attributes of the different wine-growing regions." A selfless promoter of the wines of Nova Scotia, Hans Christian even takes time out of his business day to tour visitors around the wineries of his competitors. "I'd love to see a winery in every political riding in the province," he says. In 2012, Chris Frey took over the winemaking responsibilities from Hans Christian. Chris has worked vintages in South Africa, Australia, Chile and Switzerland as well as Ontario.

Roger Dial
The Father of Nova Scotia Wine

ROGER DIAL HAS spent more than 46 years in ventures that have touched on virtually every aspect of wine culture. As an entrepreneur, he has owned and operated wineries in California and Nova Scotia, founded large-scale wine shipping and viticultural nursery enterprises and developed media/communications ventures to promote everything vinous, from the minutia of wine art to the grand sweep of "appellation consciousness." As a writer, he has written extensively for the popular wine press, drafted wine legislation and produced the occasional viticultural research report. As a wine grower, he has developed hundreds of acres of vineyards and championed high-quality cold-climate varietals (notably Vitis amurensis and L'Acadie — a French-American hybrid developed at Vineland, Ontario, as V-53261, renamed L'Acadie in homage to Roger's adopted home) against the cultural reductionism of the vinifera-only tide. As a winemaker, he has won gold medals in competitions from Bristol to New York and Toronto.

Never shy about pursuing a new wine-related enterprise, Roger and son Adam created AppellationAmerica.com in the wake of the 2005 U.S. Supreme Court decision to remove the interstate commerce barriers to direct-to-consumer wine sales. Appellation America quickly established a continental educational and distribution communications network focused on the terroir-diversity and the complex appellation structure of the entire North American viticultural world. A revolutionary concept, it was doomed as new trade barriers were thrown up, state by state, effectively leaving thousands of small wineries all across the continent barred from the long marketing reach into potential consumer interest in their terroir individuality.

Roger, who founded the original Grand Pré winery, described his pioneering efforts in the 1970s to make Nova Scotia a recognized wine-growing region. "We were full of hope that we could create a European-style wine-as-food culture — that wine would find its way to the table of everyone locally and that wine would be recognized as a viable agricultural venture." When I first visited his winery to interview him in 1982, the facility was the size of a four-car garage, and it was the only game in town. "In 10 years," Roger assured me back then, "the Gaspereau Valley is going to look like the Mosel." By the time Roger left Grand Pré and hands-on winemaking in 1988, the winery, with upwards of 60 hectares in vines, had reached a scale well beyond his original corporate plan. The challenge of his broader prophecy for the region was picked up by Hans Christian Jost and, more recently, by what Roger describes as "a new generation of young winemakers who are the equal of the best professional cadre I've worked with anywhere in the ostensibly more 'mature' wine regions of the world."

To say that Roger remains an enthusiastic cheerleader (and occasionally helpful critic)

of his province's wine industry would be an understatement. "I still keep my eye on the Nova Scotia wine industry," Roger admits. "I guess it's my paternal duty, and a prouder parent I could not be." The future of Nova Scotia's wine industry, he believes, lies in developing distinctive and consistent varietal marriages (the Tidal Bay appellation wines) that reflect their maritime terroir.

It has been my personal experience that the new generation of winemakers, of whom Roger is so proud, share that vision and are making a lasting mark on the ever-promising viticultural horizons of this unique wine-growing region.

Touring Wineries:
A Short Guide

A Year in the Vineyard

Previous spread: Burrowing Owl Estate Winery, Oliver, British Columbia.

WINE GROWERS IN Canadian vineyards tend their vines in much the same way that European farmers have done since Roman times. Admittedly, some things have changed over the centuries: The tractor has replaced the horse-drawn plow, and in larger enterprises, harvesting machines have taken over the picking where the land gradient and row spacing permit. Essentially, though, wine growing is a hands-on business in all its phases, from planting to pruning to picking.

While vines go dormant in winter, work in the vineyard is ongoing, even though there are no leaves or fruit on the vines.

JANUARY Traditionally, pruning begins on January 22, St. Vincent's Day, which honours the patron saint of vinegar makers, wine growers and winemakers. Growers prune unwanted canes to stimulate new growth and take cuttings for grafting onto rootstocks to be planted in the spring of the following year. Icewine is generally harvested in late December into January and sometimes into February, when there are sustained temperatures of minus 8°C or below.

FEBRUARY Pruning continues, though it must finish well before bud break in April or May, in order for the vines to heal. Otherwise, it's a good time for the overworked grower to go on vacation. You'll find many wineries closed this month.

MARCH If the vines have been "hilled," they have to be uncovered. Growers start plowing to aerate the soil and may also fertilize. They check stakes and trellis wires to ensure they are tight and weight-bearing. They begin to bottle last year's non-oaked red and white wines (oak-aged wines are bottled at the discretion of the winemakers, depending on how much time in barrel they decide the wine needs).

APRIL Growers take measures to eliminate weeds either through herbicides or by plowing them under. They tie canes to trellis wires before bud break. When the weather is warm enough late in the month or in May, the sap begins to rise and bud break occurs.

MAY One-year-old cuttings from the nursery are planted when soil temperatures reach 10°C. The new shoots begin to grow and often have to be contained by the use of catch wires. Growers worry about a "spring frost" at this time of year because it could destroy the fruiting buds. They begin spraying against oidium (powdery mildew) and downy mildew.

JUNE Flowering occurs in mid- to late June and lasts about 10 days if temperatures are constant at around 18° to 20°C. Growers tie down shoots and spray the vines against insects and rot. In roughly 100 days, the grapes will be ready for harvesting.

JULY In this time of vigorous growth, workers thin leaves by hand to expose the fruit to sunlight as the berries form. Some growers may thin their crop to get lower yields and so concentrate the flavours of the remaining grape bunches. They also do occasional spraying when required.

Cool-Climate Canada

Canada has been described as a cool wine-growing region. What exactly does that mean?

One definition of a cool-climate growing region is one in which the mean temperature of the warmest month during the growing season is less than 20°C. In France, growers use 10°C as a base temperature and add up the number of degrees during each day of the growing season when the temperature rises above this level. If the total is less than 1,390 degrees, it's a cool region. Ideally, wine growers prefer a long growing season that is not too warm. That allows a slow maturation of the fruit, which produces a good balance of sugar and acid and so provides a richly flavoured wine with a lingering finish. A hot growing season builds up sugars, but without cool nights, the acidity level will be low and the resulting wine will lack structure, tasting soft and flabby.

AUGUST In this month, something the French call *veraison* takes place — the berries begin to look like real grapes and change colour from green to red in red varieties or from green to translucent in white. Workers continue to weed but stop spraying. Vines left for Icewine and Late Harvest wines are netted against the birds.

SEPTEMBER Growers check sugar levels in the grapes for physiological ripeness, and early-ripening varieties such as hybrids are ready for harvesting. Growers want to pick the fruit when it is as ripe as possible to ensure a good extraction and sufficient potential alcohol. The crush pads are busy this month with the arrival of grapes at the weigh scale. Bottling of some red wines begins.

OCTOBER Harvesting of late-ripening varieties continues. Once the harvest is completed, usually by the end of the month, the vineyard is often plowed, most specifically to force the roots of young vines to penetrate the soil more deeply. Some wineries use the pomace (grape residue) from their winemaking to spread back on the vineyards as fertilizer. October is one of the busiest months in the cellar, with the crush (breaking the skins so the fermentation starts) and the pressing of the grapes (to extract the juice).

NOVEMBER Growers bank the soil against the base of the vine stocks to protect them from a deep winter freeze. They may also spread any minerals and nutrients that are needed at this time. The onset of colder weather shuts down the vine, and it becomes dormant until spring.

DECEMBER Workers remove the year's shoots by pruning; otherwise, December is a quiet month in the vineyard. Unless an early cold spell demands the harvest of Icewine, growers draw up their holiday wish lists and think of warmer climes.

Timing Your Winery Visits

Summer

If you're interested in getting acquainted with the vines before you sample the wines, this is the best time to visit a winery. Many wineries have guided tours that take you into the vineyards to show you how they grow grapes and how they protect the vines during the winter months. Be prepared to deal with traffic, both pedestrian and vehicular.

Fall

Harvest time seems to be the favourite period for most wine tourists, especially when the leaves are changing colour. Keep in mind that this is also the busiest season for the winemakers — they may not have time to discuss the merits of their wines with you. If you plan to visit with a group, phone ahead and alert the winery personnel. And make sure to check up on their parking facilities, given the crowds through September and October.

Winter

If you don't mind driving in snow, you can catch the winery staff in mid-winter harvesting their grapes for Icewine, or the cider makers in Québec gathering frozen apples for Ice Cider. Call ahead to find out when the wineries intend to pick, as harvest dates vary from year to year. You might even find yourself co-opted into helping.

Spring

The snow may still be on the ground, but it's maple syrup time, and you will have the opportunity to visit and taste at the many sugar bushes and *cabanes à sucre* as well. The vines begin to sprout in May, so don't expect to see much from the vineyards or inside the wineries unless you're fascinated by bottling lines at work.

A dramatic view of the Similkameen Valley from the Seven Stones Winery.

Winery Etiquette

Bouchons Bistro in Kelowna, B.C., above, showcases Okanagan wines. Opposite: Colleagues at Nova Scotia's Blomidon Estate Winery — Bria MacNeil, Simon Rafuse and Travis McFarlane — enjoy a break.

RUNNING A WINERY and vineyard is a year-round business, but the tasting rooms at many wineries are open only during the summer season from May to October or in November. Rather than turning up on the doorstep to find a "Closed" notice on the door, call ahead or check the website for the winery's hours. If you are travelling in a large group, phone earlier and advise the tasting room about your arrival time. The weekends are their busy time, and if you want special treatment as a group, ask if there is a private tasting room. However, if you want to ask the staff questions, my advice is to avoid visiting wineries on holiday weekends. They'll be too busy to give you much individual attention.

Don't block access to doorways or to your fellow visitors with your car. If you're cycling, make sure you park your bike so that no one will back over it. Many wineries now have bike racks.

You will be greeted with open arms as long as you are there to sample the wines and not to party. Most wineries don't charge for a sample pour and will be happy to serve you up to four selections. (You may have to pay for their specialty wines, such as Icewine.) It is *de rigueur* for professional wine tasters to spit, so don't be afraid to follow this custom. Spittoons and dump buckets are provided, but make sure your aim is true. And don't feel you have to finish each sample. You won't offend the tasting-room staff if you dump

the sample after one sip. Keep your opinion to yourself and move on; the wine you find too dry may be perfect to the taster standing next to you.

Don't start with Icewine and then try to taste a Sauvignon Blanc, because the initial sweetness will make the wine that follows taste sour. Begin with the dry white wines, move to the dry red wines, and finish with the Late Harvest and dessert wines.

If you're on a guided tour, don't carry on a conversation with your friends/partner/strangers while your guide is explaining the winemaking process. And don't monopolize the guide's attention by asking too many questions; others may have questions too. Avoid touching anything to see whether it's working or if it's full (don't knock on barrels or tanks), and keep your eyes open for hoses or anything else that's lying around on the ground. Be sure to close doors after you: Wines have to be kept at a cool temperature.

Sign the guest book, if there is one. This way you can receive information about the winery's upcoming events. Tour the wine store and pick up some wine. You will find a much better selection here — older vintages, small lots, experimental wines — than you will find at any liquor store or even the winery's off-premise stores. There's an old joke: How do you make a small fortune in the wine business? Answer: Start with a large one. Remember, wineries are in business to make money. To show your gratitude for a tour and tasting, pick up a bottle or two of your favourite wines on the way out. The winery earns more by selling directly to you than it does by selling the same wine through the liquor board stores. It would really like to sell all its wines across the counter.

Three Steps to Tasting

WINE APPEALS TO all five senses: sight, smell, taste, touch and hearing. But for the most part, you're using the first three — in that order as well — when judging the quality of a wine. The first sensory response you have is to the colour of the wine, then to its smell, as you lift the glass to your nose, and, finally, to its taste.

Step 1: Sight

HOLD THE GLASS against a white background or a good source of light. The wine should look clean and bright. Study the colour and tilt the glass so that you can see the rim where the wine touches the glass. Young wines hold their colour to the rim; older wines begin to fade at the edge. White wines start life as white as water and gain a golden colour with age. Red wines begin as a deep purple and lose colour over time. Browning edges in a red wine are a warning sign and suggest age or oxidation. A browning of the yellow of white wine suggests maderization (oxidation that gives a sherry-like flavour to the wine).

Swirl the glass and watch the transparent wet residue on the sides form into tears, or legs, and slide down the glass. This residue is the alcohol in suspension on the side of the glass. The thicker and more slow-moving these legs, the higher the alcohol content.

Step 2: Smell

Swirl the wine in the glass. This action causes the esters that carry the wine's aromatics to evaporate and rise. You'll get a more concentrated bouquet by swirling. You can tell 75 percent of what you need to know about a wine "on your nose." The bouquet will tell you what the wine will taste like; the only thing it won't tell you is how long the wine will linger on your palate.

Look for faults first. Are there any off-odours, such as the smell of vinegar (volatile acidity) or prunes (oxidation) or damp basements (corkiness)? The wine, depending on the variety or blend, should generally smell of fruit, flowers, sometimes vegetables (especially Sauvignon Blanc), and it will have the scent of vanilla or coconut, toast and smoke if it's been aged in oak.

Step 3: Taste

Take a sip and let the wine wash over your entire palate. The first sensation you'll notice is the wine's sweetness, because the taste buds that register sweetness are on the tip of the tongue. As the wine works its way to the back of the mouth, you'll experience acidity (a lemon-like flavour) and, in red wines, a slight bitterness caused by tannin, a natural compound found in the skins, pits and stalks of grapes. Tannin is a preservative that allows red wines to age. Astringent when young, the tannins soften with the years and, eventually, in old wines, will precipitate out as sediment.

Feel the weight of the wine in your mouth. High-alcohol wines, whether red, white or rosé, will be full-bodied and mouth-filling. Low-alcohol wines will feel light-bodied. Ask yourself if the wine is in balance. A great wine will be seamless: The fruit, acidity, alcohol, oak and tannin will be perfectly in harmony. If the wine is over-acidic, over-oaked, highly tannic or shy on fruit, it will be unbalanced. You should not be able to pick out one particular element of its composition if the wine is well balanced.

A wine taster's secret: Suck in air when the wine is in your mouth. You'll extract more flavour, just as you get more of the wine's bouquet by swirling it in the glass.

Index